AF292329

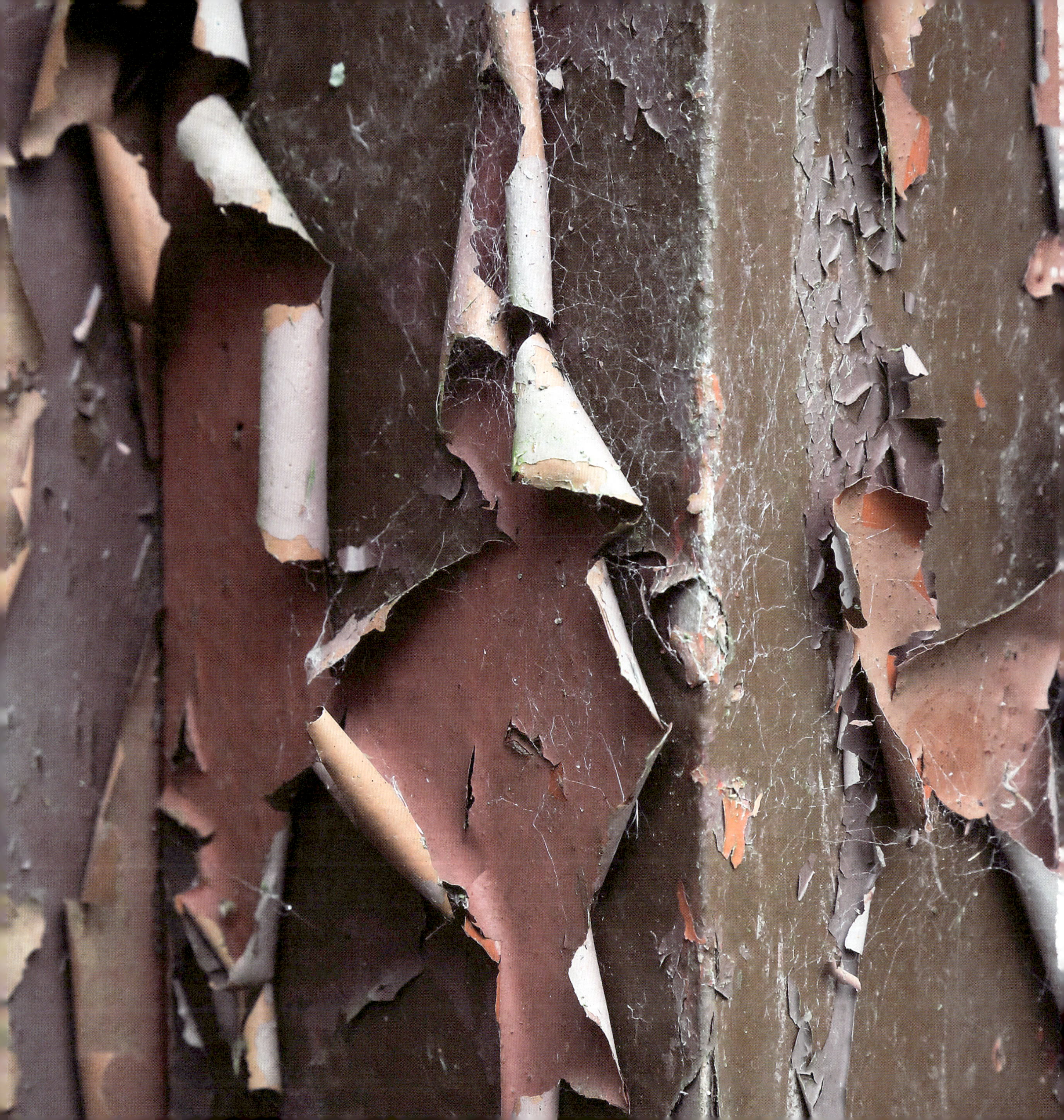

PEELING PAINT AND RUST

DAVID WILSON

BIRD EYE BOOKS

FOREWORD

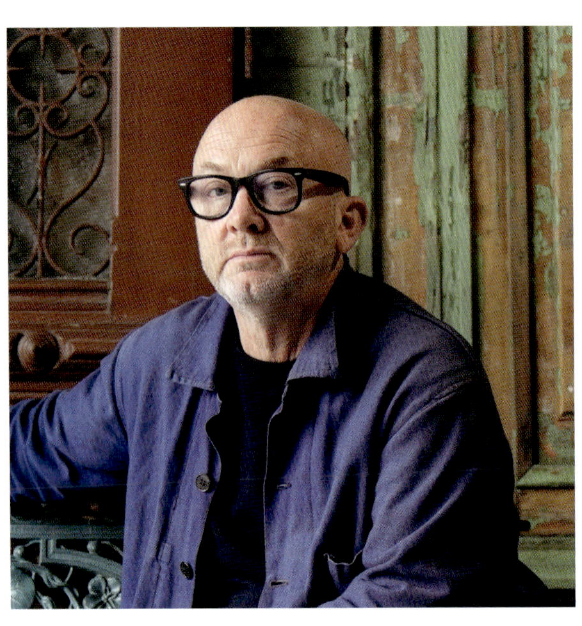

Drew Pritchard

I've spent much of my time being fascinated by things. Whether it is a building, a car or a piece of furniture, I have almost always found a unique beauty in dereliction and decay. My strange attraction to these forgotten things was clear to me even as a child roaming the abandoned buildings in and around our small village on the coast of North Wales. The things I remember: the flaking paint of a corrugated chapel roof, Stan the Butcher's tatty shop sign and a Ford Zephyr which never once left the front yard of the local garage. Being a child, I did not understand where this fascination came from. In fact, I probably rarely questioned it at all.

In adult life, I have tried to answer this question a few times. Here's my best attempt. Fundamentally, that intangible feeling which links all these things is the promise which a dilapidated item holds; ideas of what it could be and what it was. In turn, these ideas allow your imagination to take hold of the item and run with it. The things they have seen, the passing decades they have witnessed, and how on earth did they remain so untouched? That history will always hold a certain charm. Perhaps there's something romantic going on there too. The one thing I do know for certain is that these naturally occurring, never-ending processes of decay are valuable beyond anything you or I can summarise in pounds. Unfortunately, longevity and robustness are principles no longer cherished by the always-brand-new, single-use culture which we find ourselves in today.

I am certain that David Wilson understands how valuable these ageing, crumbling things are too. In fact, the series of photographs which make up the following pages may convince every reader of the necessity of preserving that which others may overlook. Wilson places the eroded, the rust-bitten and the slowly fading away front and centre throughout these images, almost as if they were portraits. In this way, Wilson illuminates the extremely characterful nature of these places and these things. Whether focusing on detail shots or taking in wider, landscape-like captures of a building's crumbling facade, Wilson finds a good deal of humour in these images too. Rust-covered grills flash toothless grins and colourful doors ignore the otherwise sombre tone of a past-its-prime entranceway. Perhaps taking inspiration from fellow Welshman Dylan Thomas, Wilson's images serve as a celebratory obituary to those too-stubborn-to-crumble things which refuse to go gently into that good night.

Drew Pritchard

INTRODUCTION

Many years ago, I read an article about the import of Volkswagen campervans into the UK from California, the self-proclaimed 'golden state' – California that is, not the UK. These vans were rust-free, or pretty much so, even though they were twenty, thirty, or more years old. It seemed that the climate from whence they came was kind to the bodywork.

I live in Wales, and Wales, unlike the golden state, isn't kind to bodywork. In fact, Wales isn't kind to any object or structure located outdoors that has been painted or is made of metal. You see, Wales has proper weather. Brutal on occasion. The kind of weather that degrades our best efforts at preservation of the built and manufactured environment. Paint peels and metal rusts in outdoor Wales.

Our weather is served up primarily from a westerly direction, from the Atlantic – wet and windy. Sure, Ireland shields us a little, and we must thank it for that, but the sideways rain and blustery squalls batter Wales all the same. Painted surfaces bubble and lift. Metal oxidises. Perhaps this process of weathering is more noticeable in Wales as we've taken one particular building material as our own – corrugated iron. Cheap and versatile, it's been used extensively from the nineteenth century to the present day for the erection of sheds, garages, houses, chapels and all manner of structures, big and small, the odd outdoor toilet – or *ty bach* (little house) – too, as it happens. We Welsh love this crinkly material and you won't travel far without seeing some manifestation of its use.

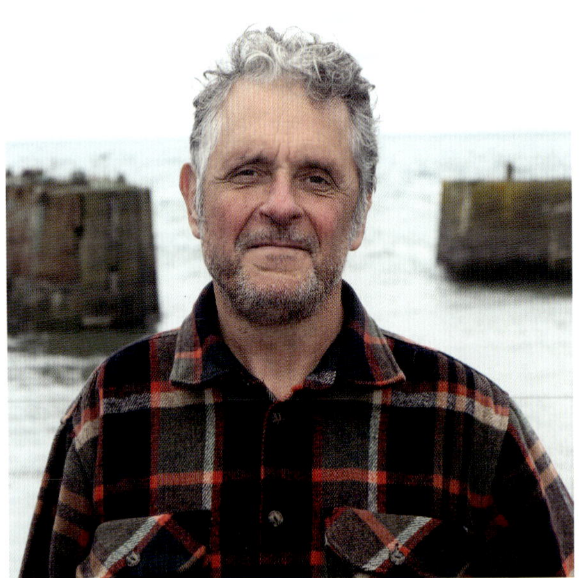

David Wilson

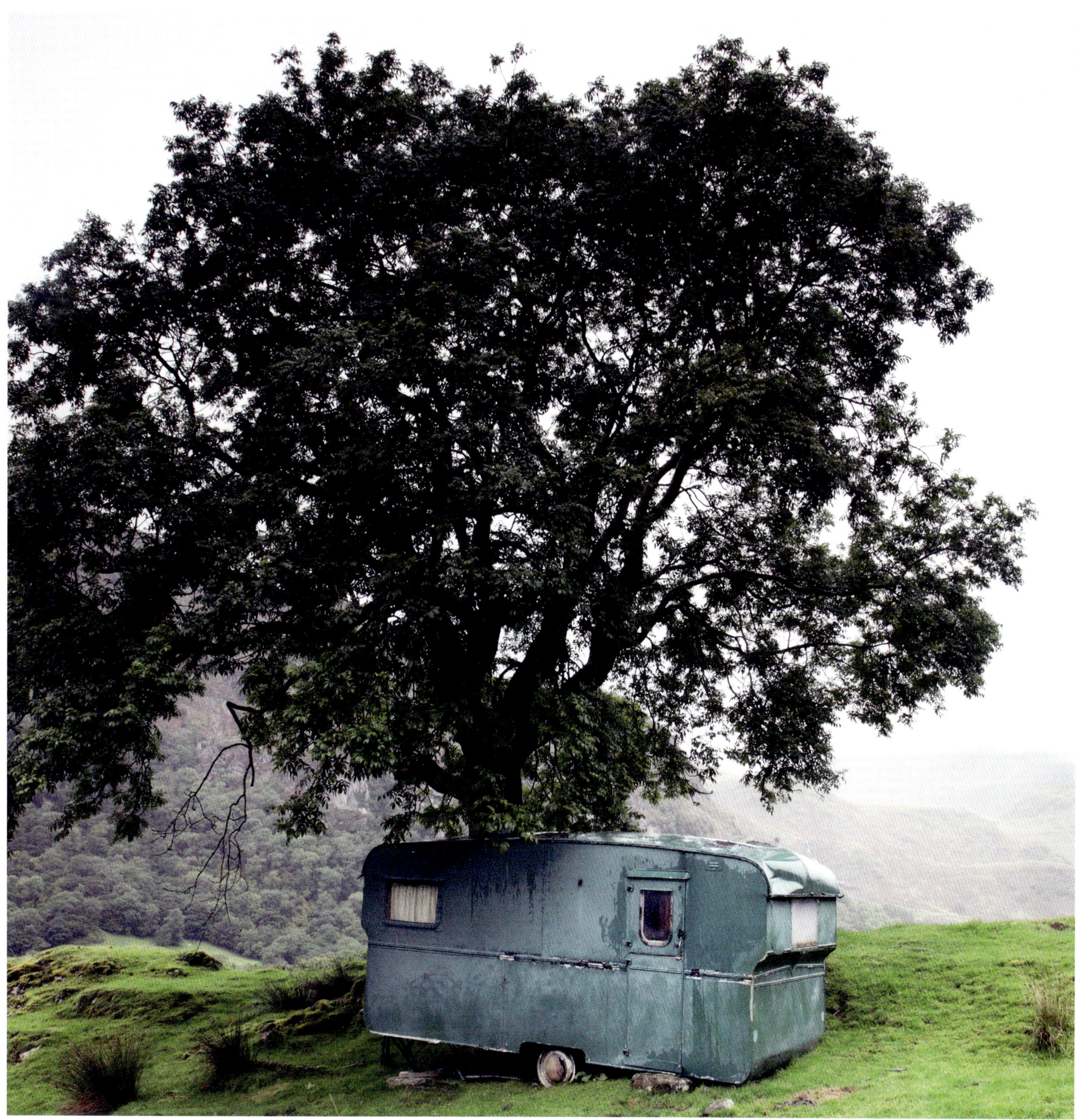

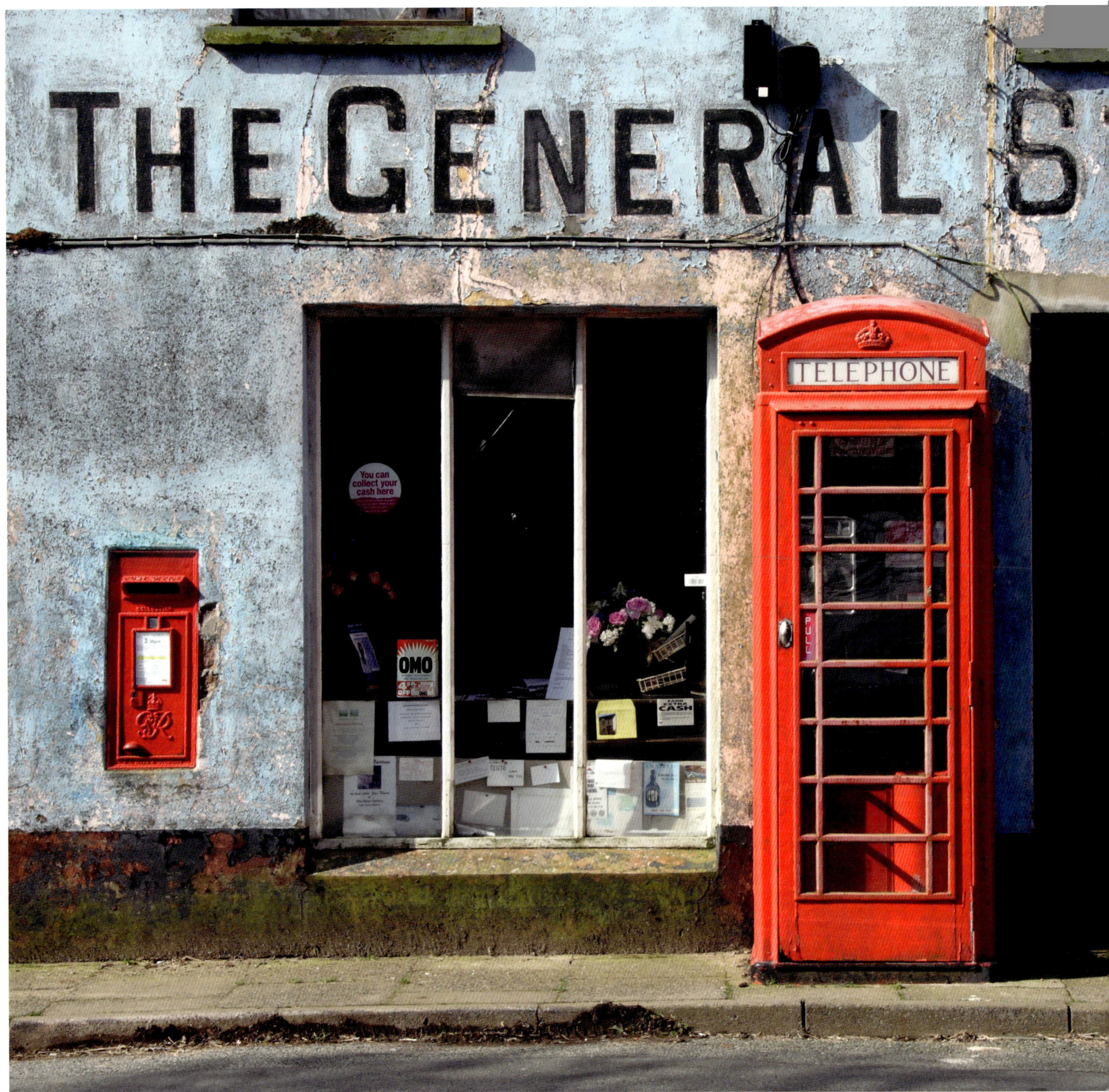
THE GENERAL S
TELEPHONE
You can collect your cash here
OMO
CASH

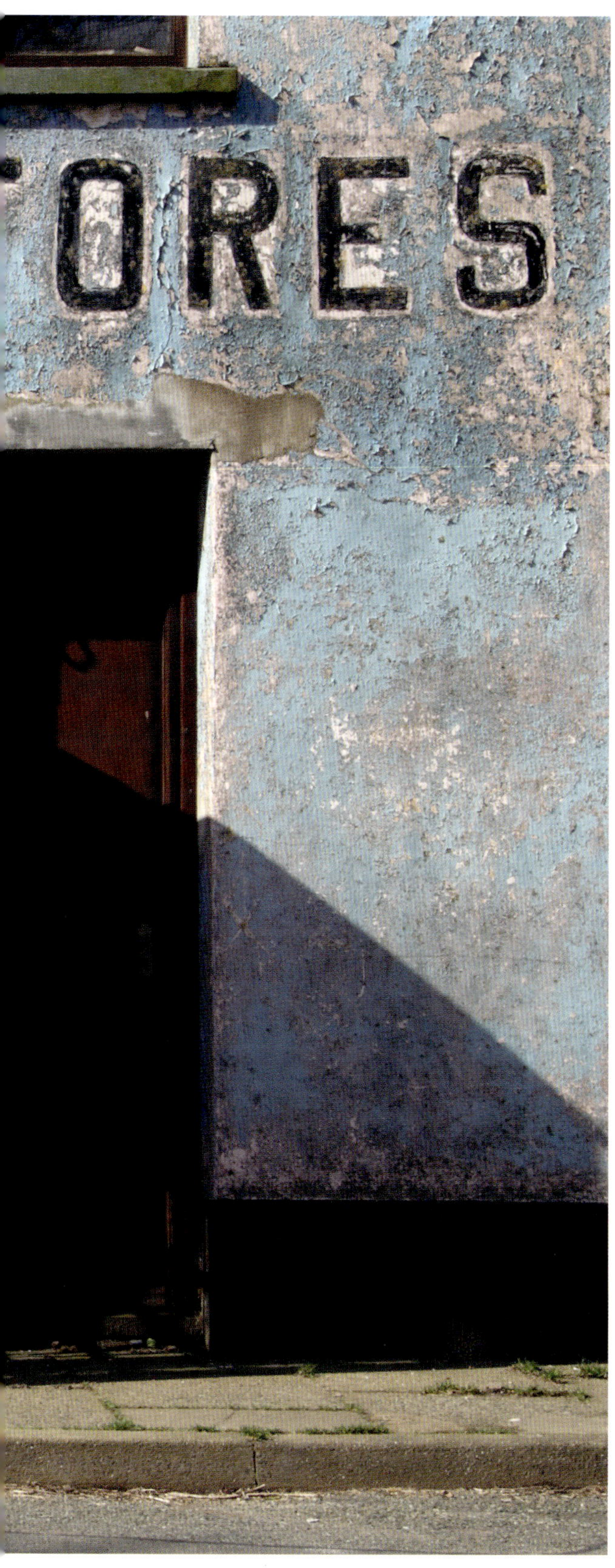

In the near twenty years that I've been fortunate enough to take photographs for a living – when photography has been my job – I've indulged a passion for black and white landscape and documentary photography. I've produced many books, courtesy of a very indulgent publisher, photographed in my beloved black and white. Perhaps troubled minds prefer tones to colour! The evocation of mood. The dark and the light. The extremes. The narrative element inherent in a monochrome image.

On my travels around Wales compiling portfolios for various projects – monochrome book projects – I kept bumping up against a nagging realisation. You see, I kept encountering the beauty of decay and found that I was rather drawn to it, and I was torn, as the language of decay is colour. What else could it be? The peeling paint and rust of outdoor Wales presented itself to me and I enjoyed capturing it. Of course, I resisted any notion that these colour images I was collecting could amount to anything. They were surely no more than interesting interludes in my quest for the perfect black and white photograph. But I kept discovering decay, deriving joy from framing and capturing it, and, more importantly, I began to look out for it. Search for it even.

Left: Mathry, Pembrokeshire, 2010.

There was an aesthetic beauty to these images of decay I was
photographing, like three-dimensional works of art in the landscape.
Installations, if you like, in art-speak. But there was also a sense of
sadness, as I felt that I was documenting a dislocation in the rural
communities of Wales – a dying way of life. The world, as ever, moves
on and it seemed to have left these places and their objects behind, as
they struggled to keep up with the globalisation of life – that suffocating
homogeneity of big business with its determination to strip us of choice
and condition us to see what they offer as progress. Really? And what of
the village shops and garages that have shut? The small farms that can
no longer be profitably farmed? The siphoning of young people to the
bigger towns and cities? Yes, but what about the convenience of online
shopping, the multi-nationals would say, and, who can resist the time-
saving ease of the weekly shop at the supermarket? Most of us are guilty
of it, if guilt is the right word. Keeping it local is not always as easy as we
might imagine. Our village shop closed recently, in a village where there
has been a shop for over one hundred years. Many reasons were cited,
one of which was a lack of customers. I miss our shop. I miss the chats
and the laughter. And the gossip, of course.

It's becoming increasingly difficult to find these graceful studies in decay,
as people are inclined to tidy things up. Put things right. That obsession
with neatness and order. Too many house makeover programmes on the
television perhaps. Such a shame, though, as that slavish conformity
is robbing us of interest in the landscape. Robbing us of opportunities
to reflect on what went before. To look and touch and remember what
people once strove to make and build, these decaying monuments to past

endeavours that, in many instances, have outlived those that made or built them. Get out there and experience them while you can. It's fun; a bit like archaeology, but with the treasure above ground.

One rainy day I trawled through this archive of decay, curious as to what I'd accumulated over such a long period. Nearly twenty years of drive-by shootings! They sparked affectionate memories of past book adventures, providing snapshots of particular moments doing the thing I love. But this collection also seemed to hint at something cohesive. Something that hung together as a whole. They seemed to tell a story, and I thought, 'They could make a book.' And, thankfully, my publisher felt the same. This resultant book is testimony to a two-decade labour of love for the peeling paint and rust of Wales. I hope you take as much enjoyment from it as I did while making it.

David Wilson

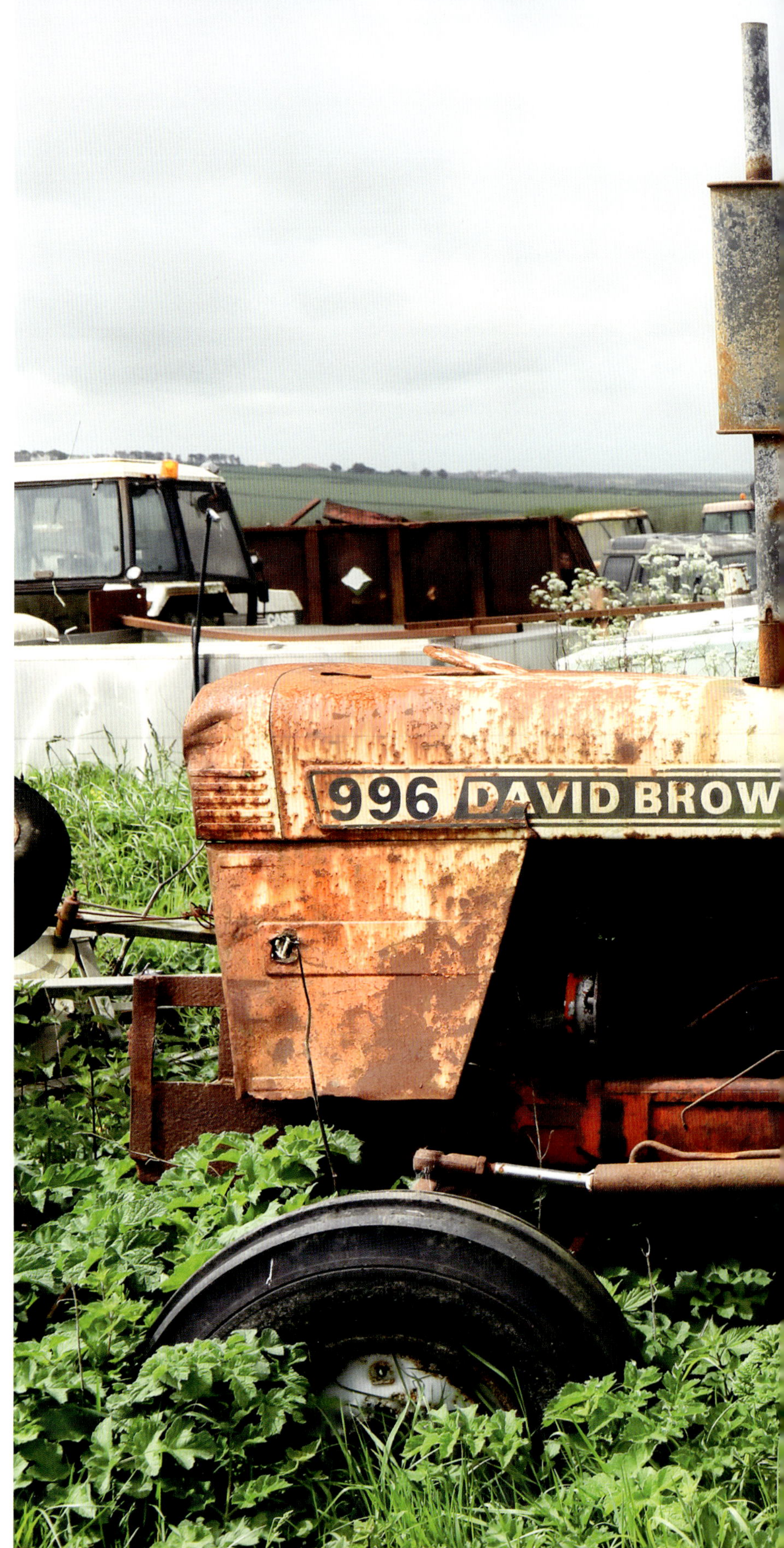

Pembrokeshire, 2022.

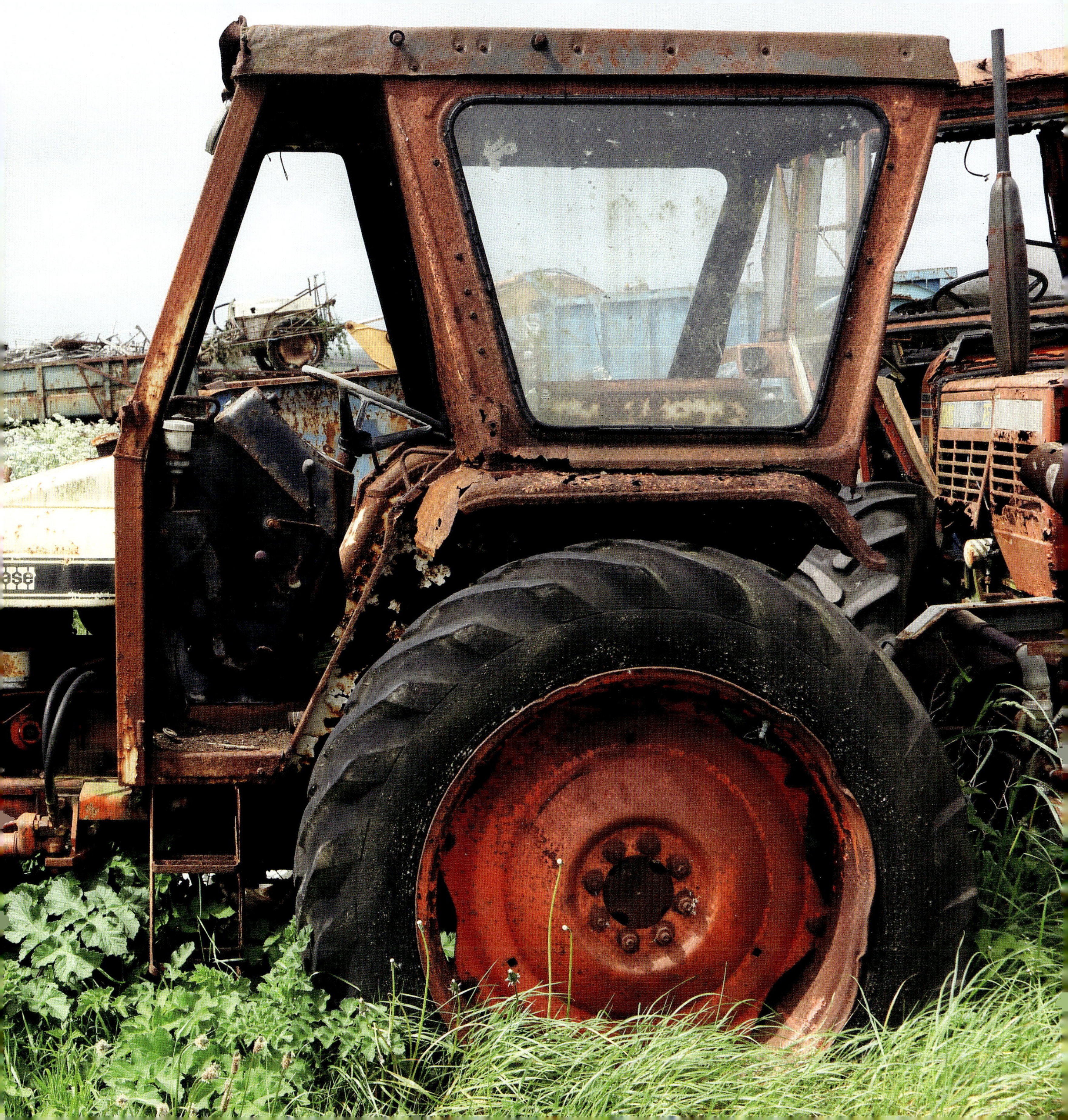

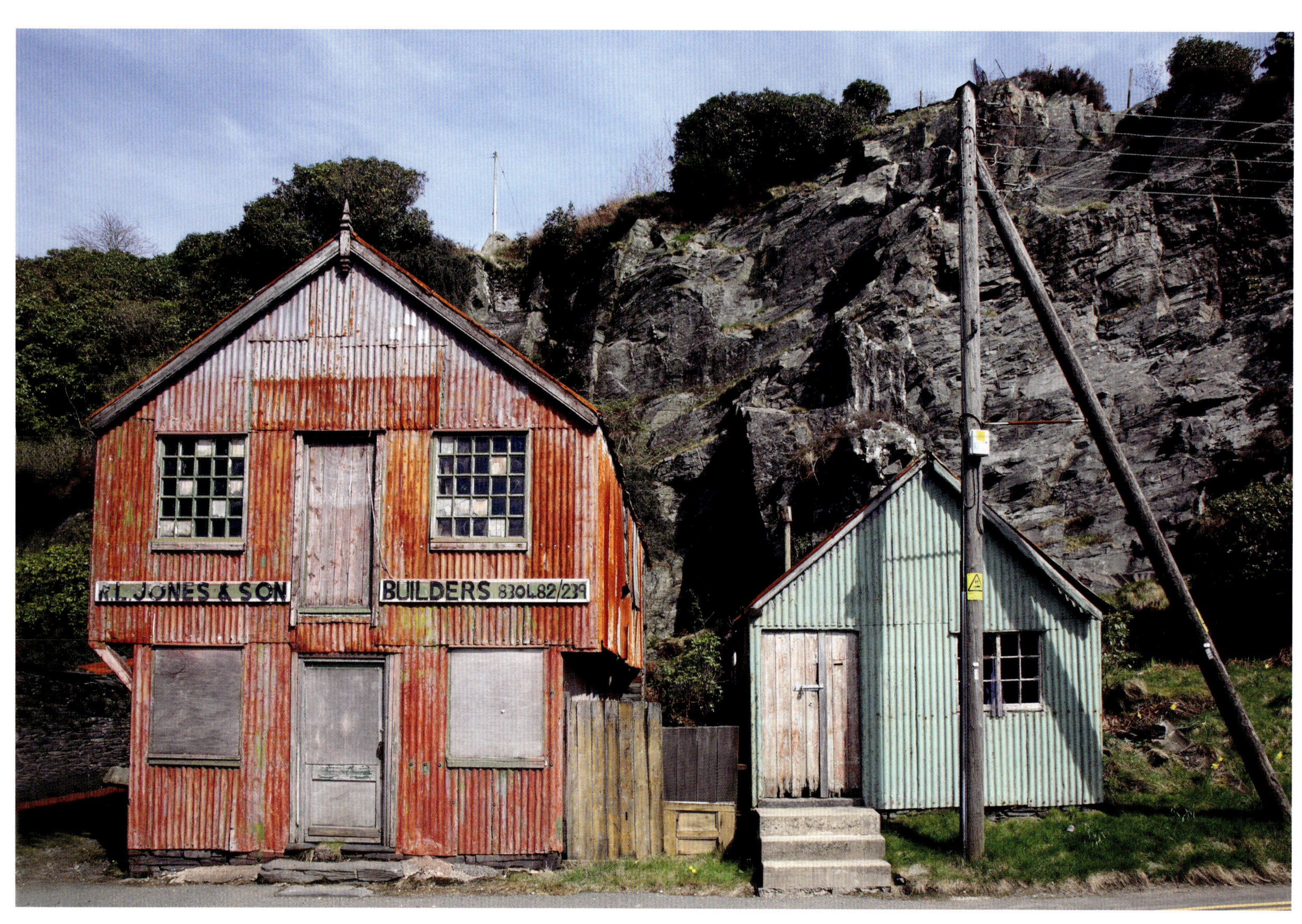

Above: Blaenau Ffestiniog, Gwynedd, 2011.

Right: Middle Mill, Pembrokeshire, 2022.

Pages 14-15: Llanrug, Gwynedd, 2012.

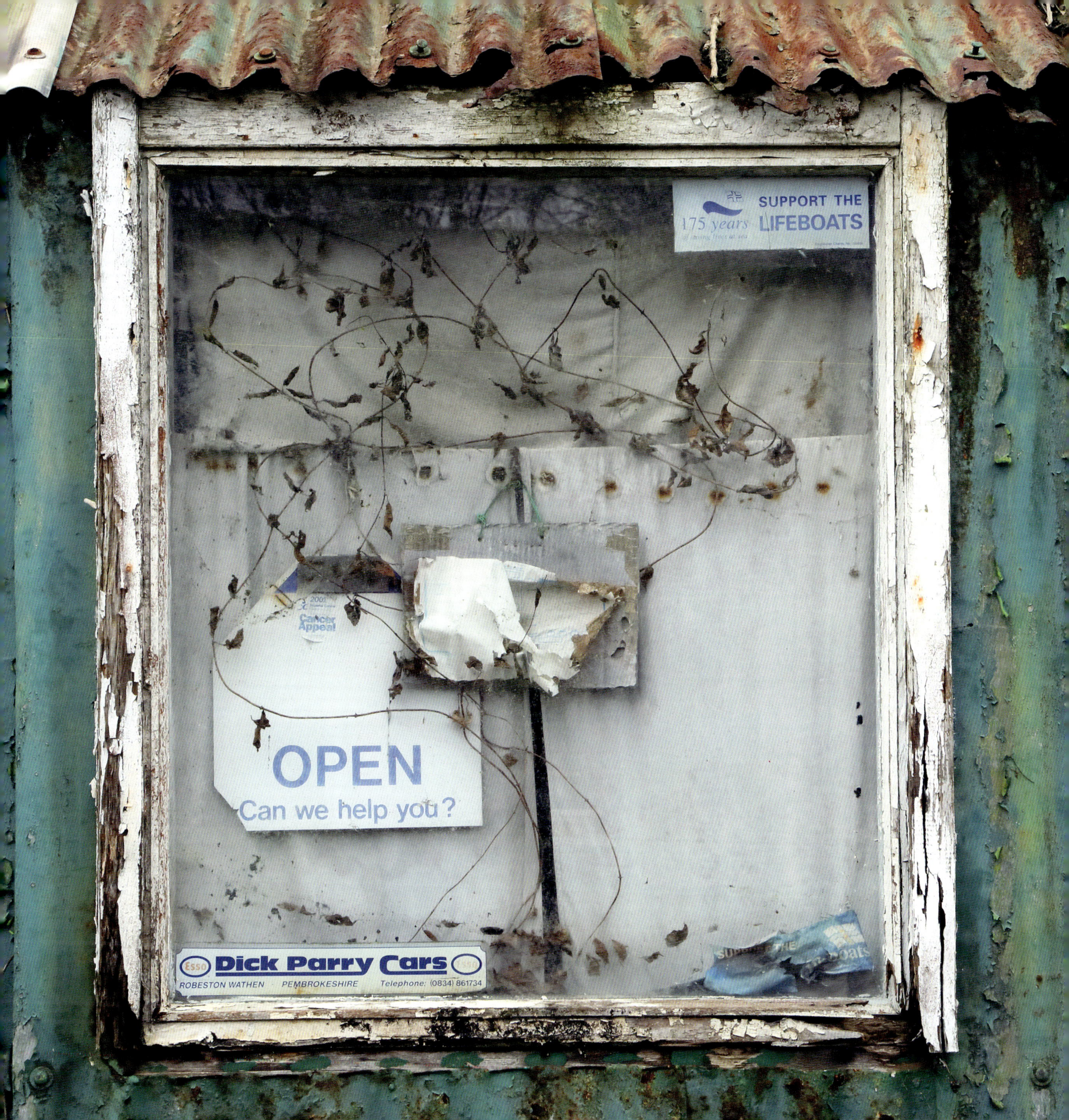
175 years
SUPPORT THE
LIFEBOATS
Cancer
Appeal
OPEN
Can we help you?
Dick Parry Cars
ROBESTON WATHEN · PEMBROKESHIRE · Telephone: (0834) 861734

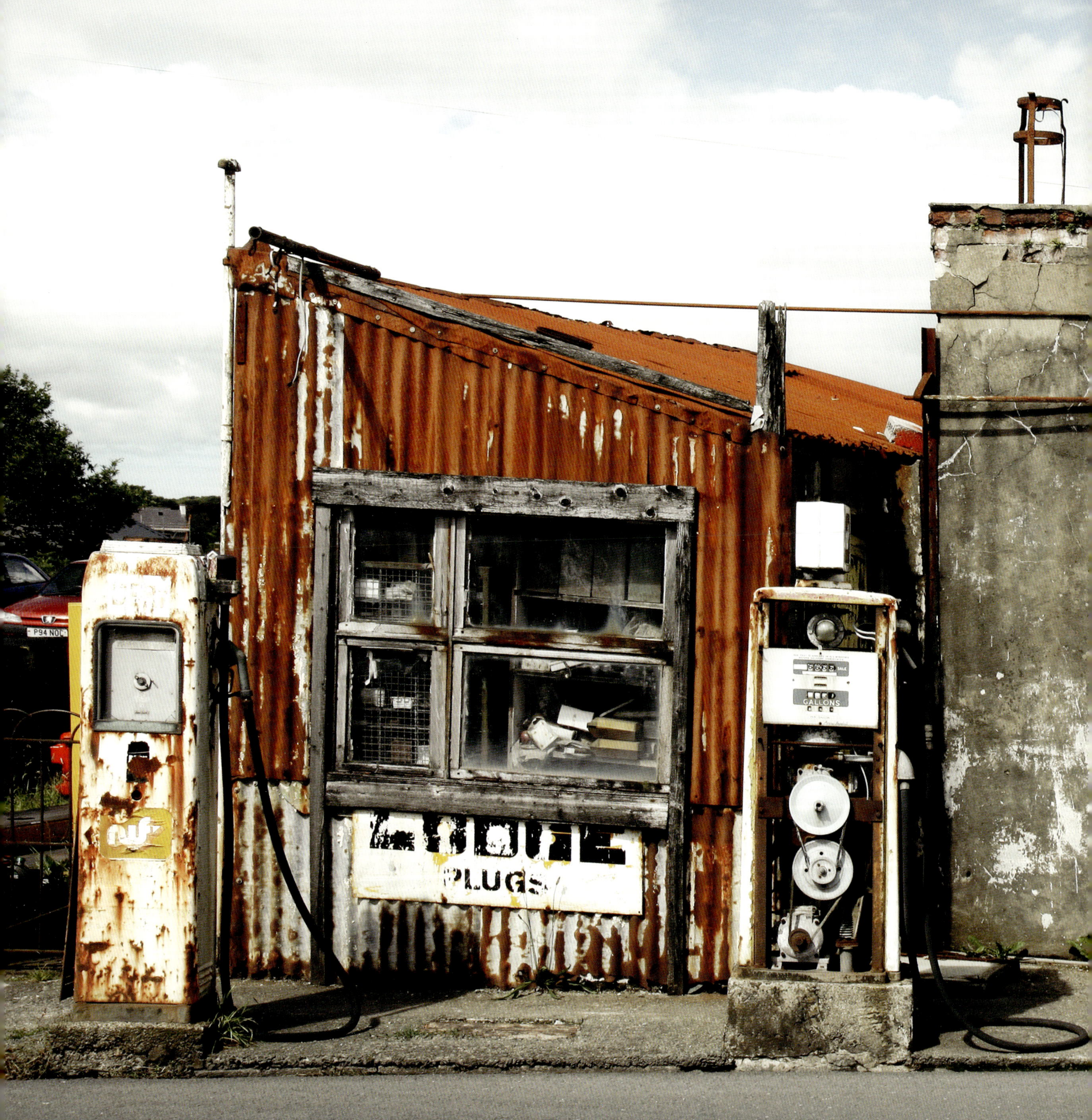

PLUGS
GALLONS
P94 NOC

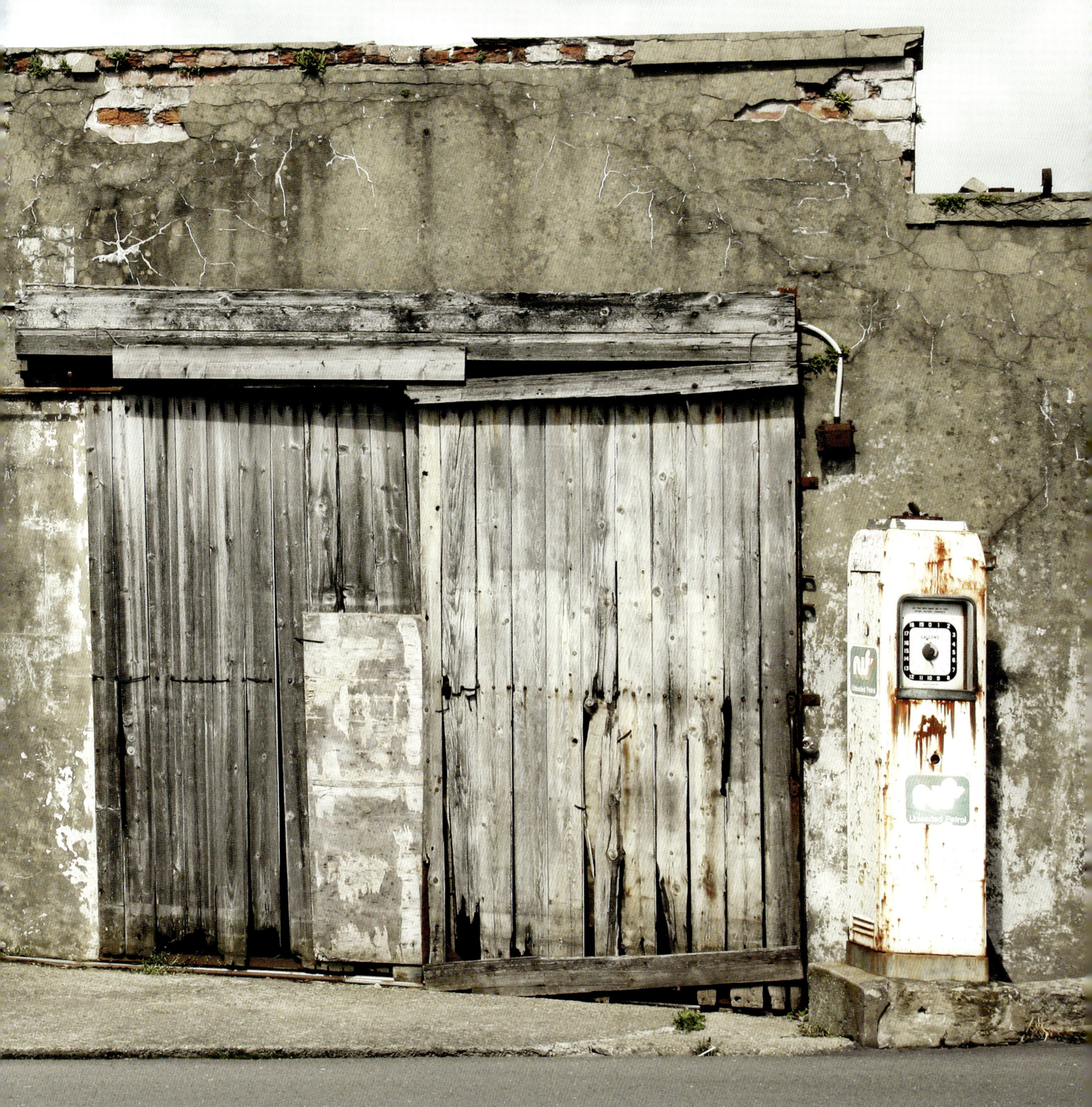
GALLONS
Unleaded Petrol
Unleaded Petrol

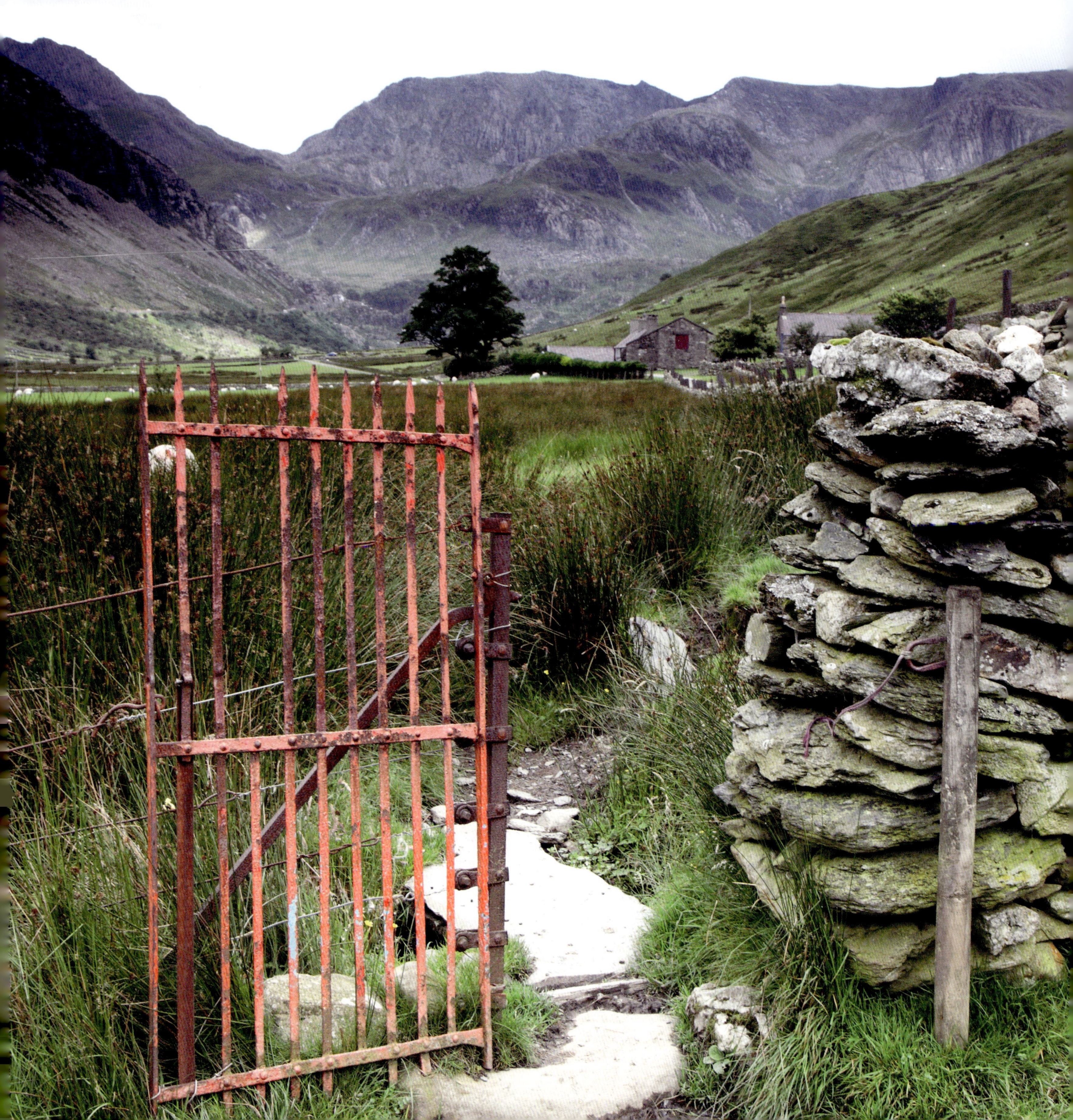

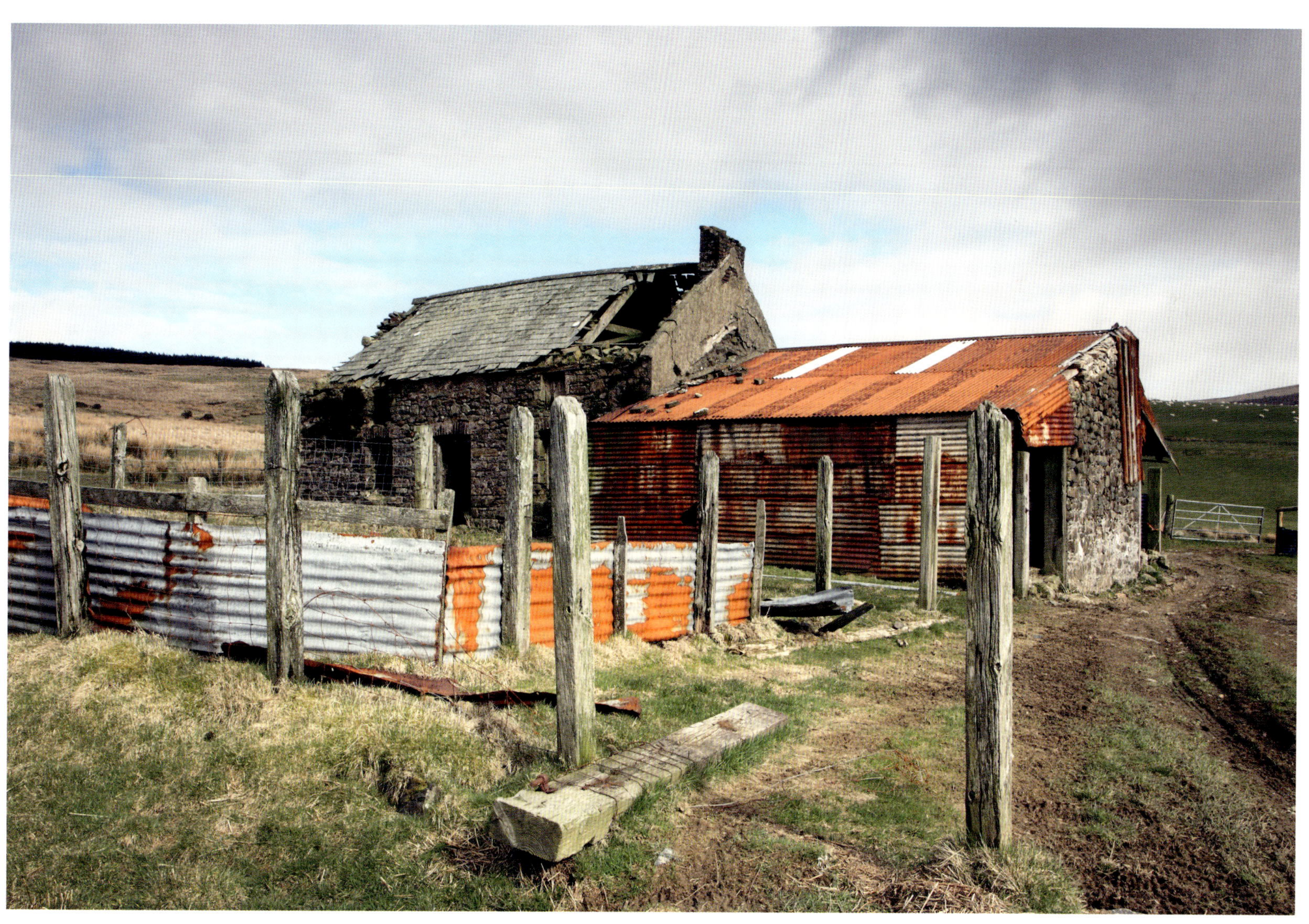

Left: Ogwen Valley, Snowdonia National Park, 2012.

Above: Preseli Hills, Pembrokeshire, 2008.

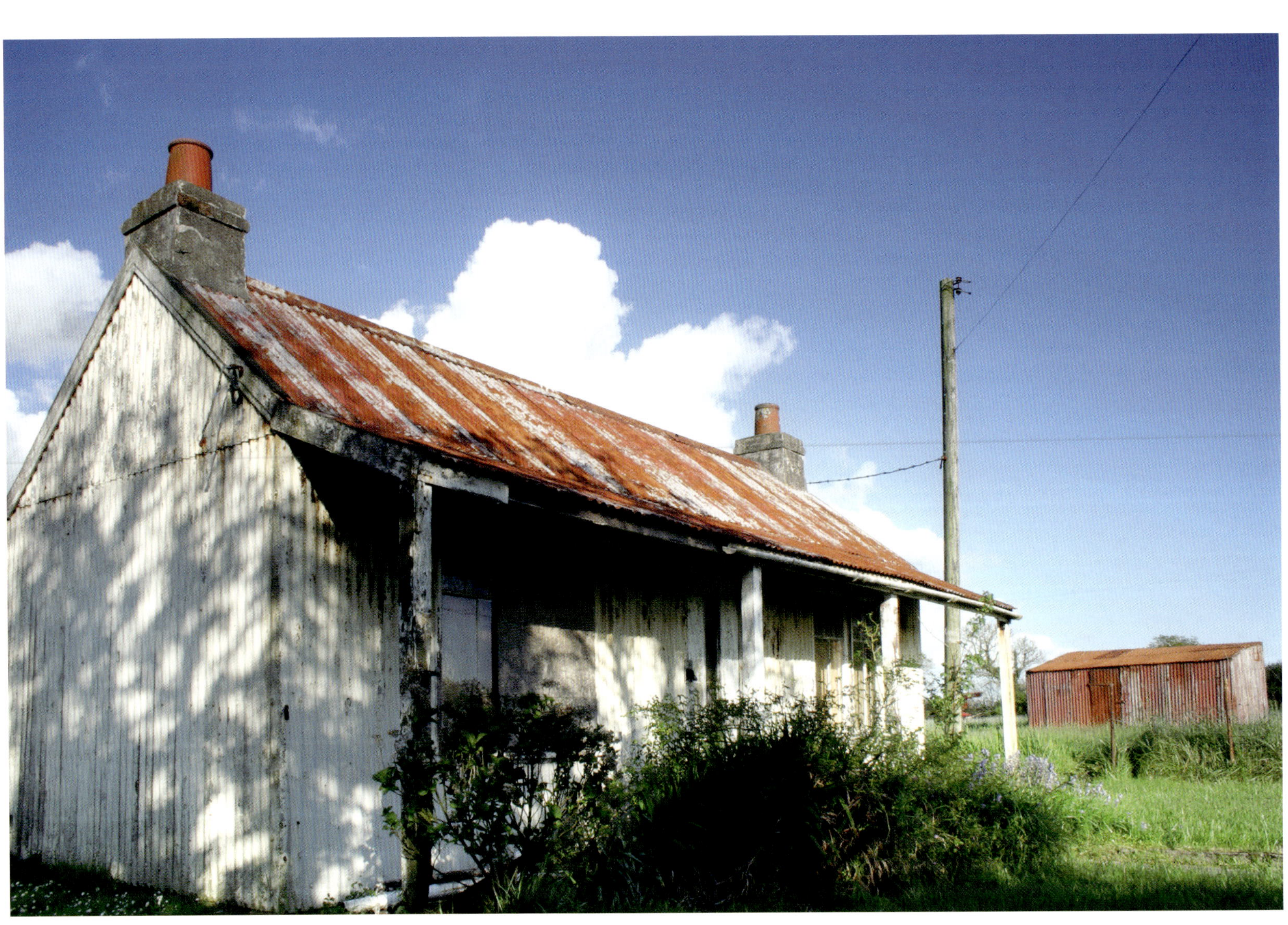

Llangwm, Pembrokeshire, 2004.

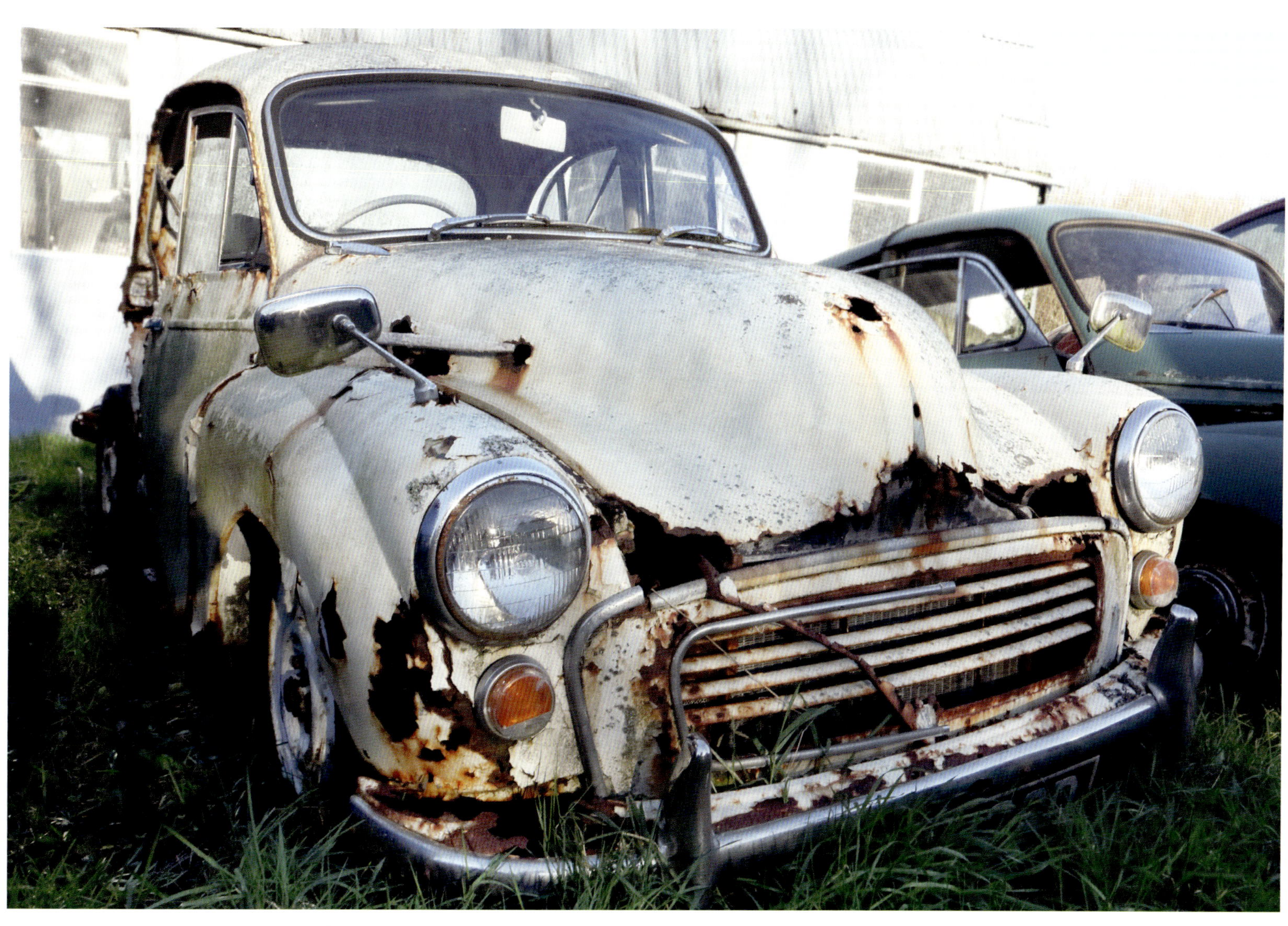

Pontiago, Pembrokeshire, 2023.

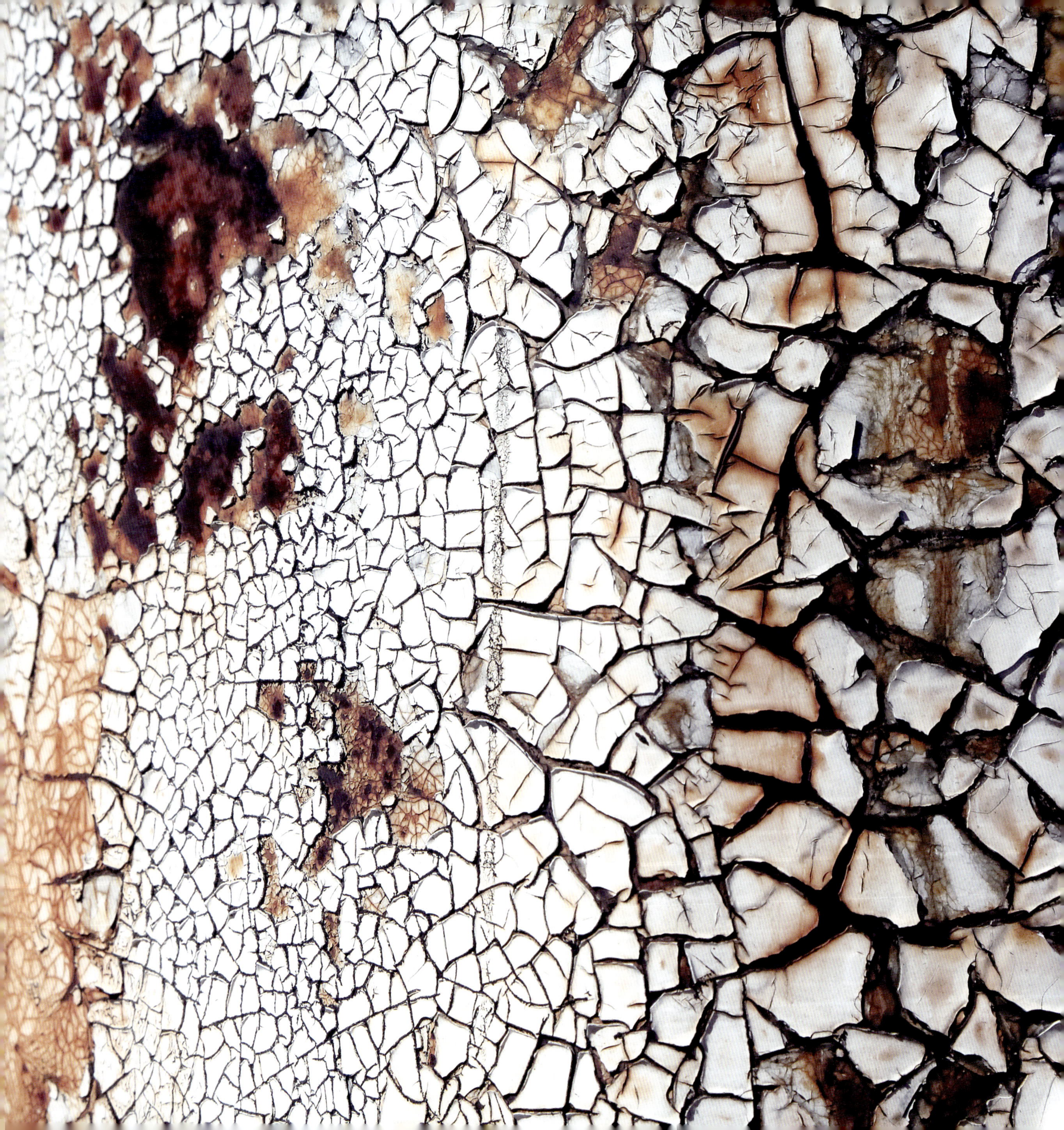

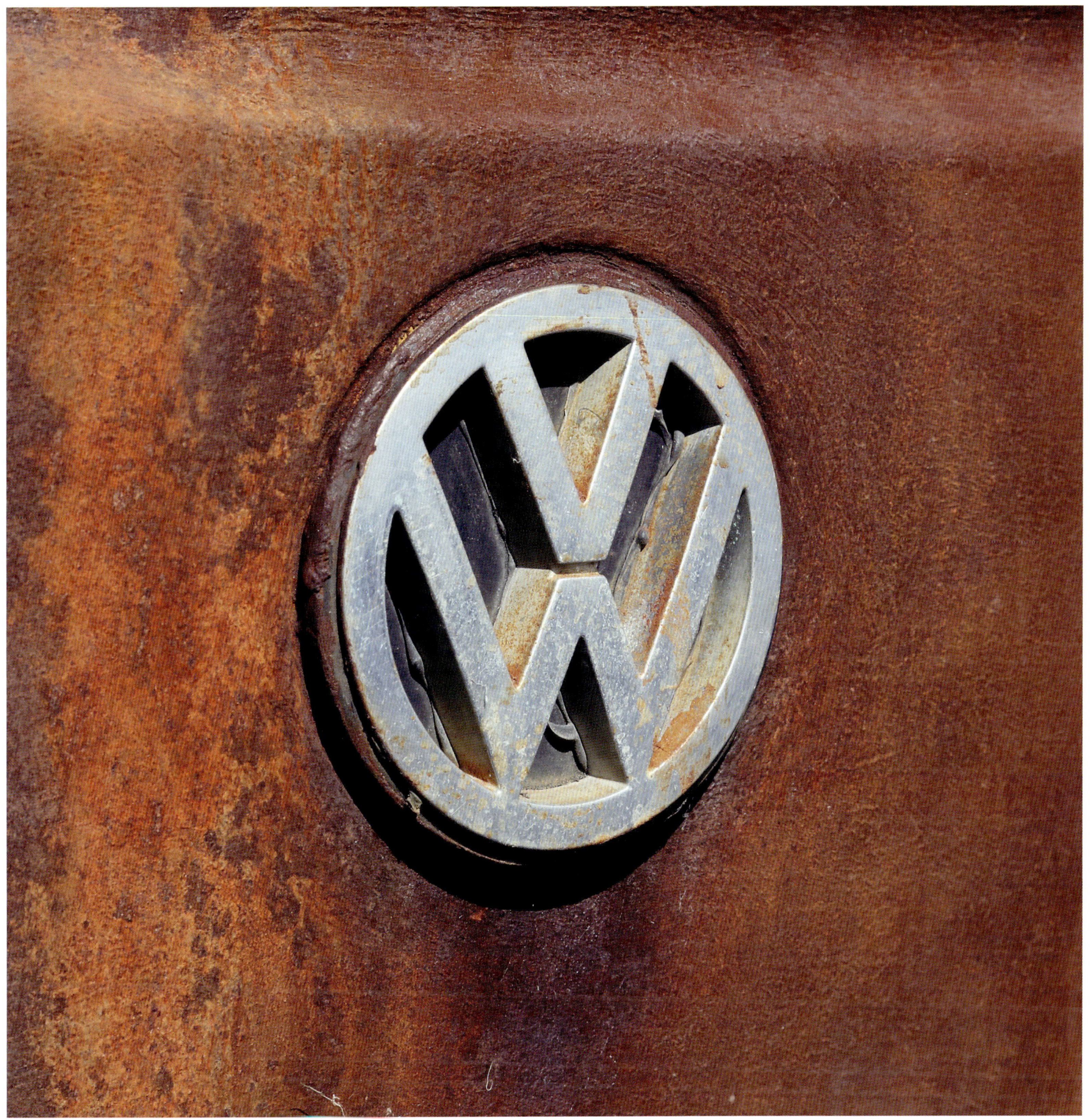

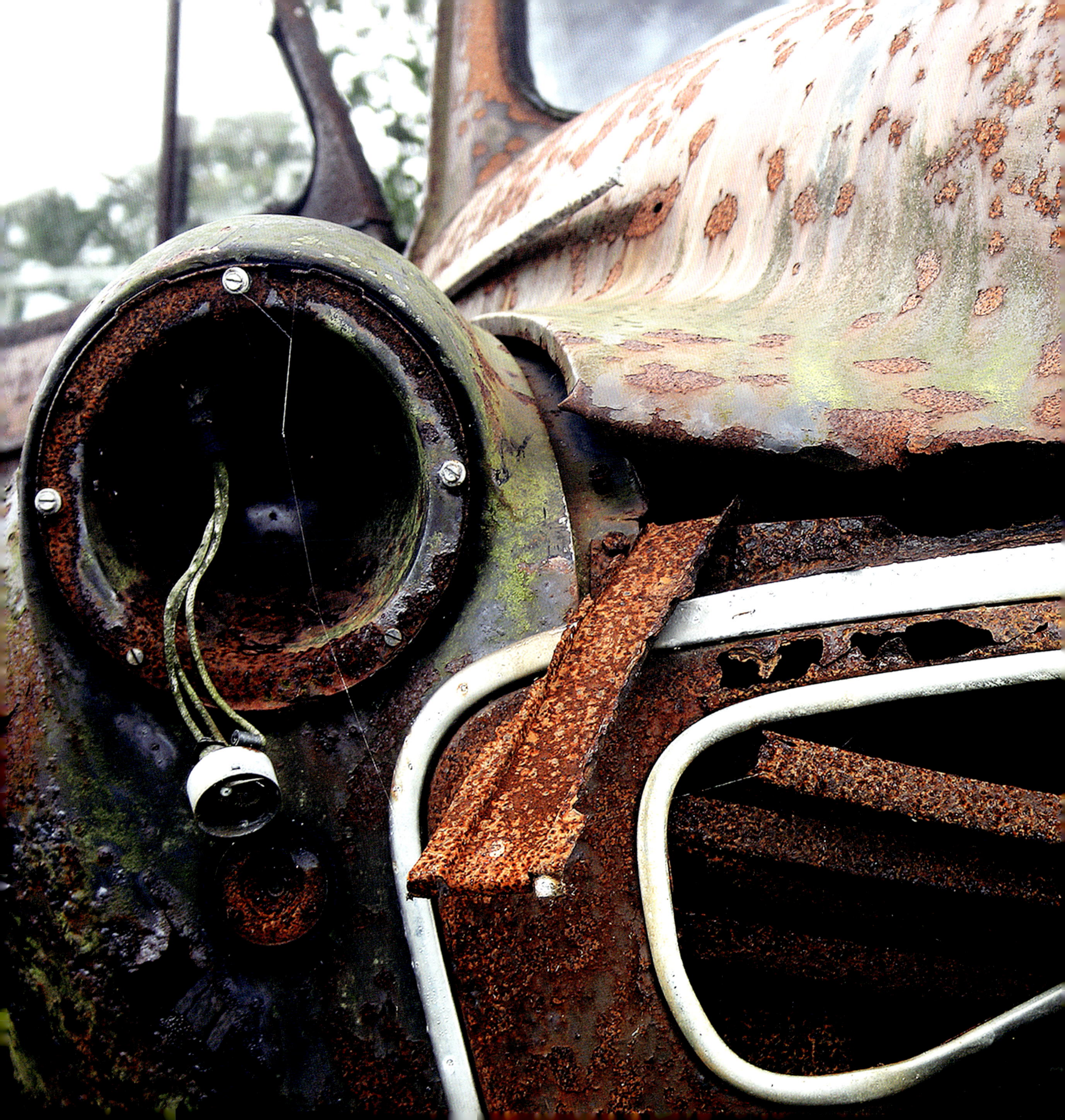

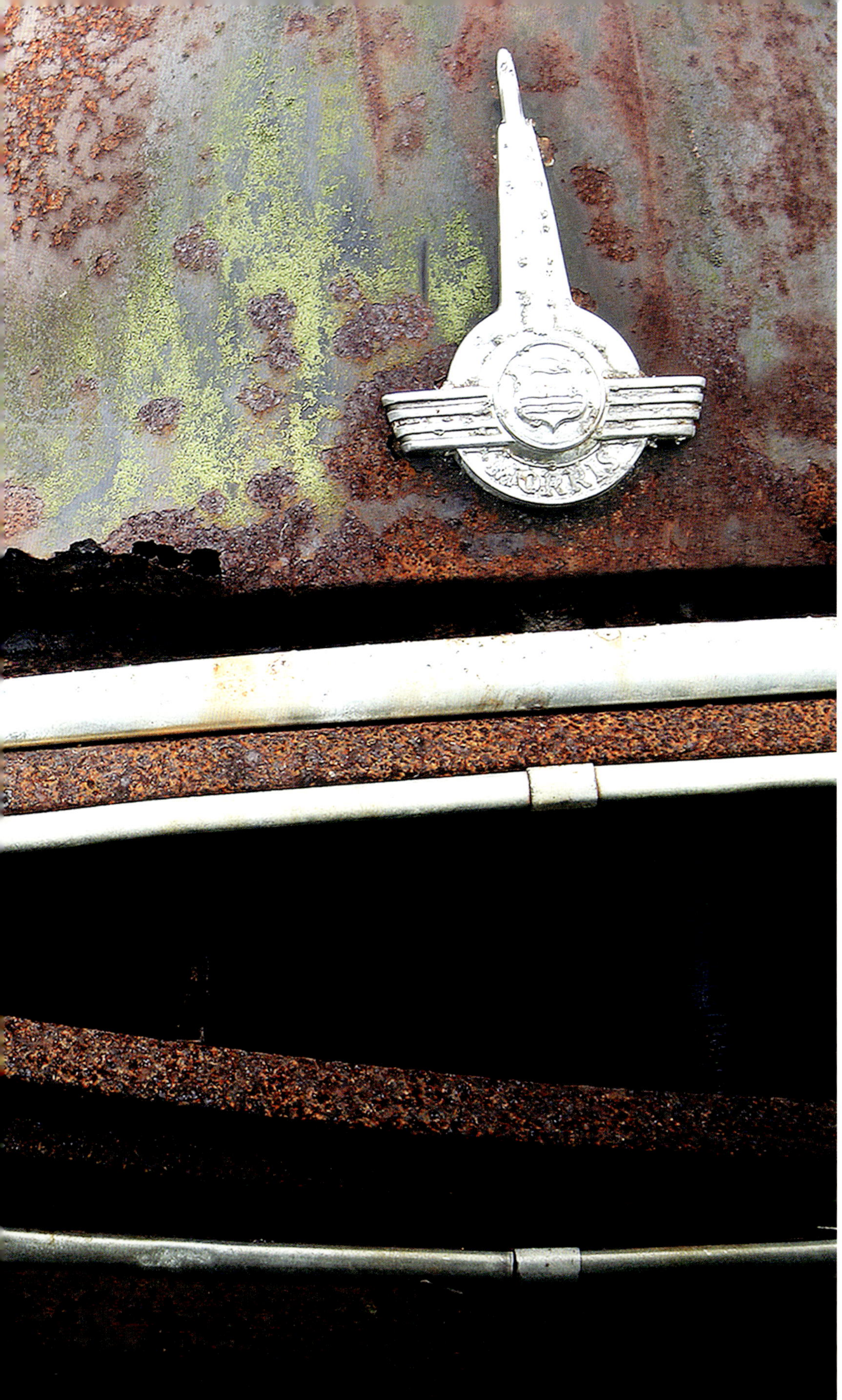

Pontiago, Pembrokeshire, 2004.

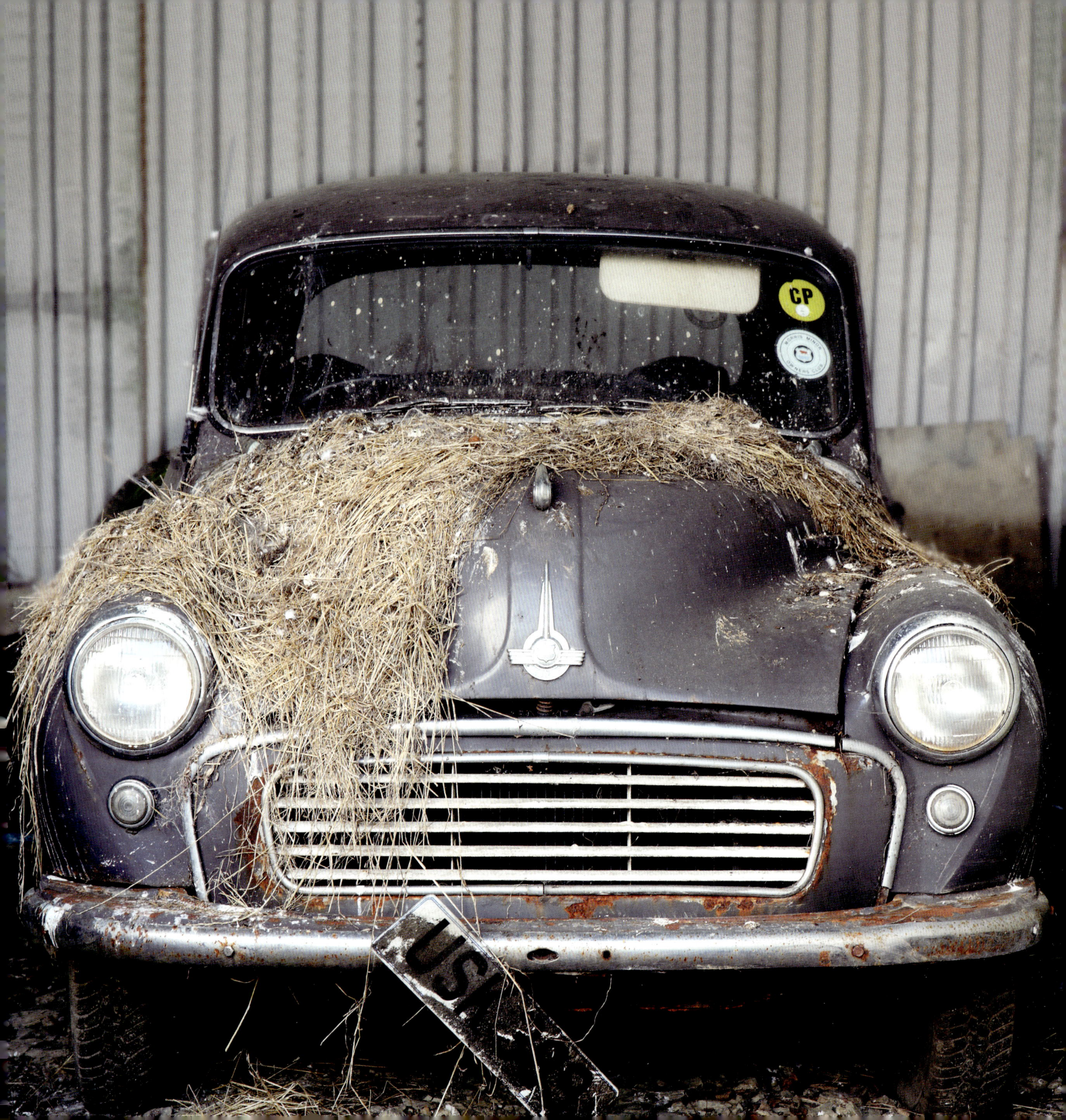
CP
US

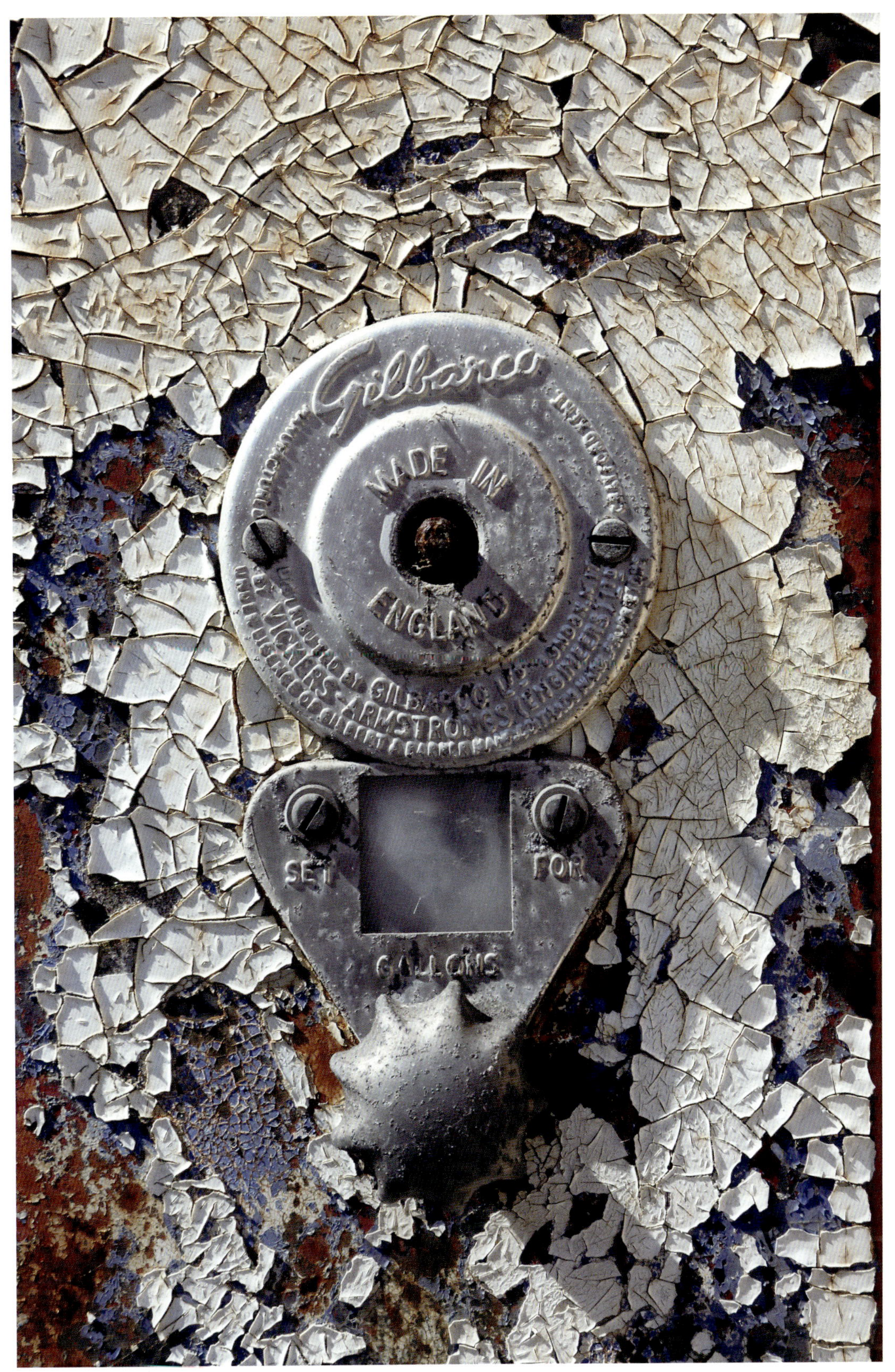

Left: Wiston, Pembrokeshire, 2008.

Right: Cardigan, Ceredigion, 2023.

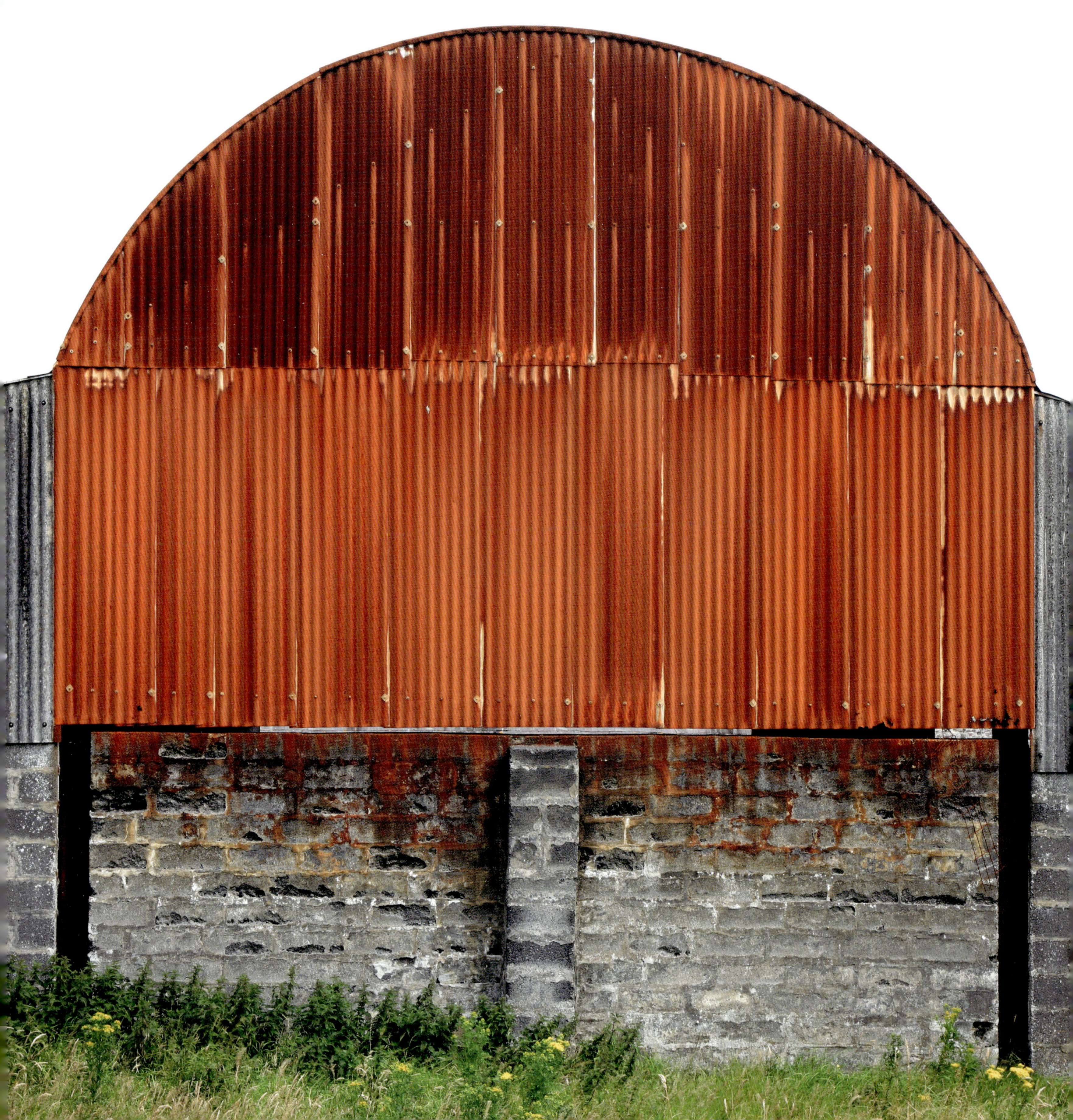

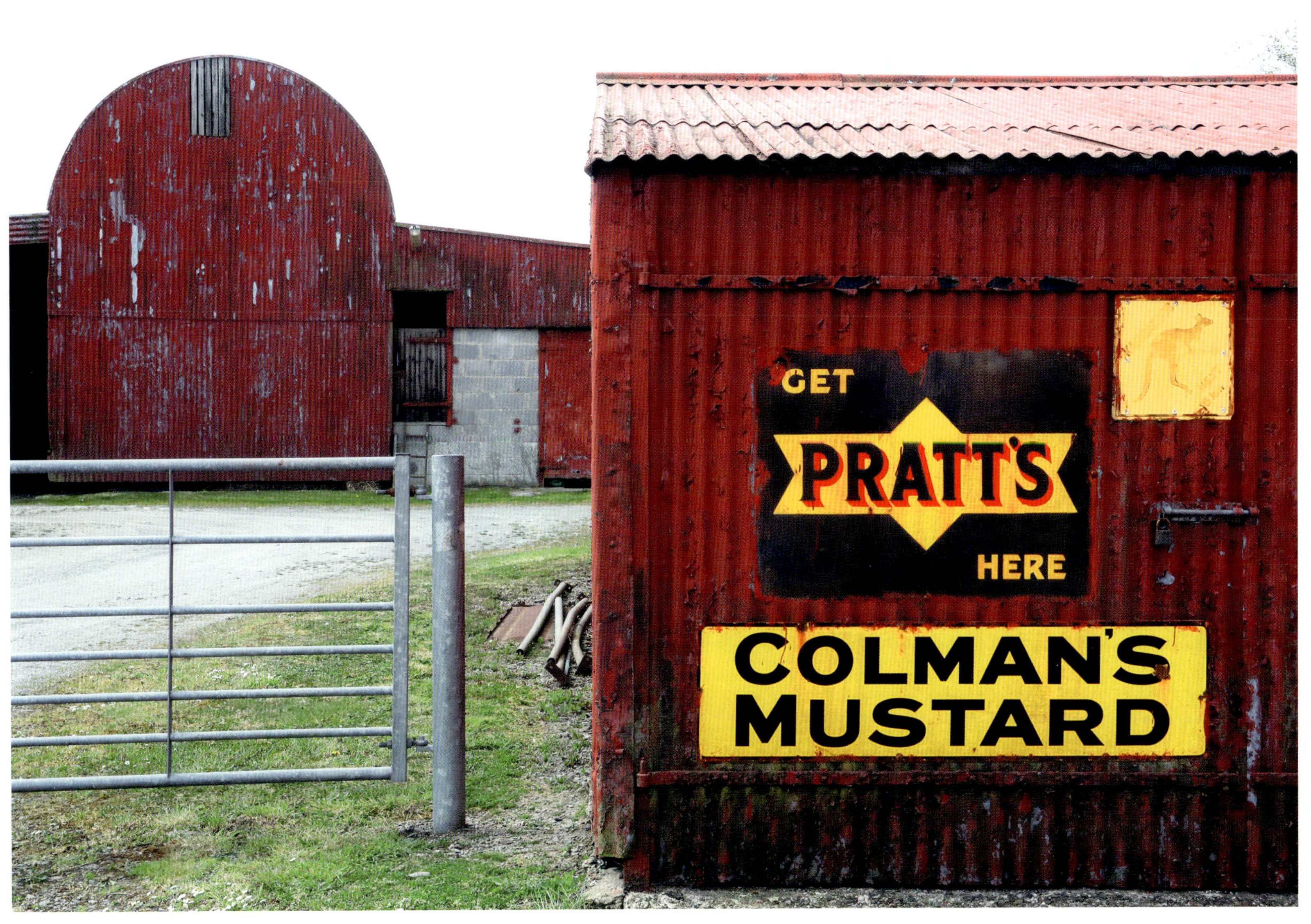

Left: Laugharne, Carmarthenshire, 2009.

Above: Ceredigion, 2016.

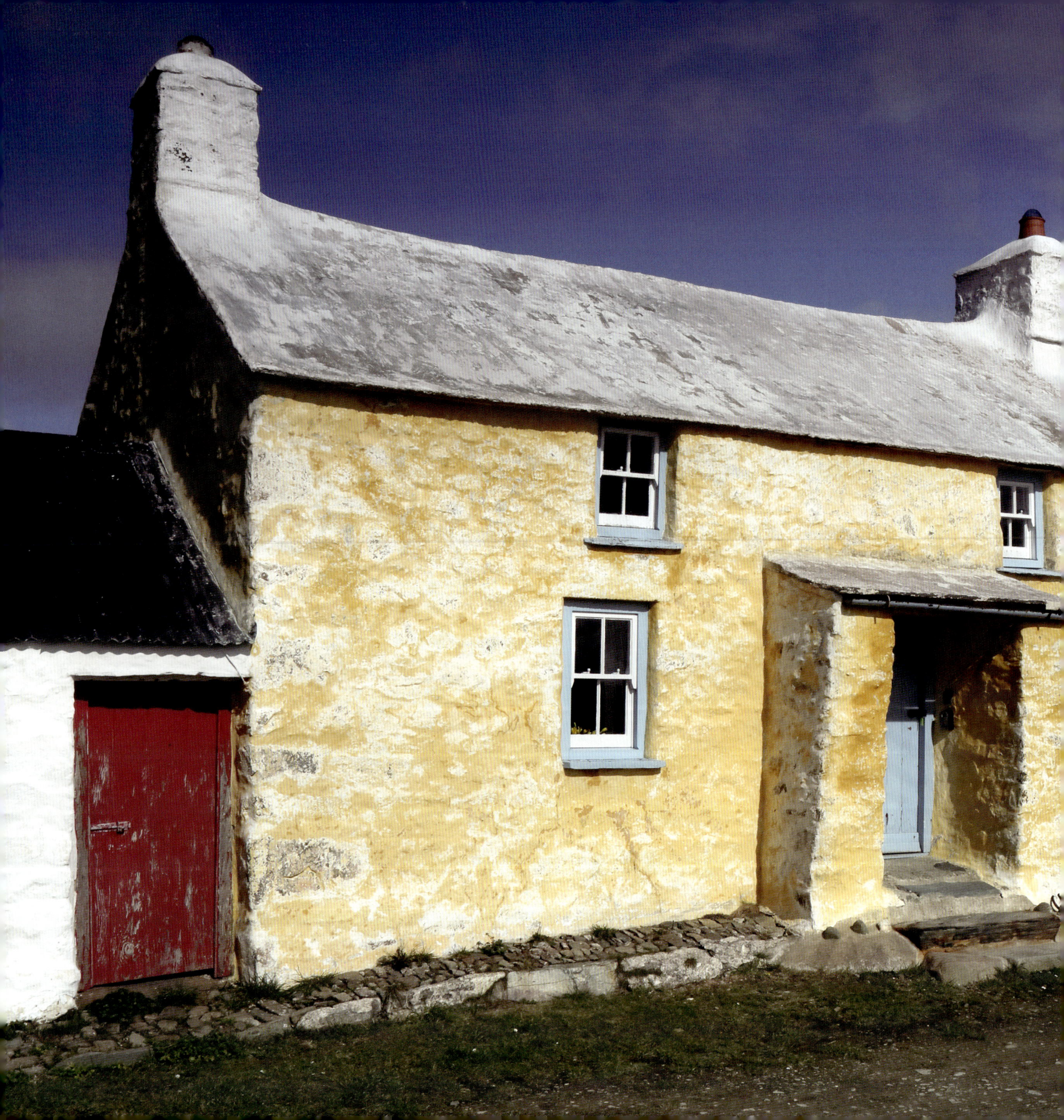

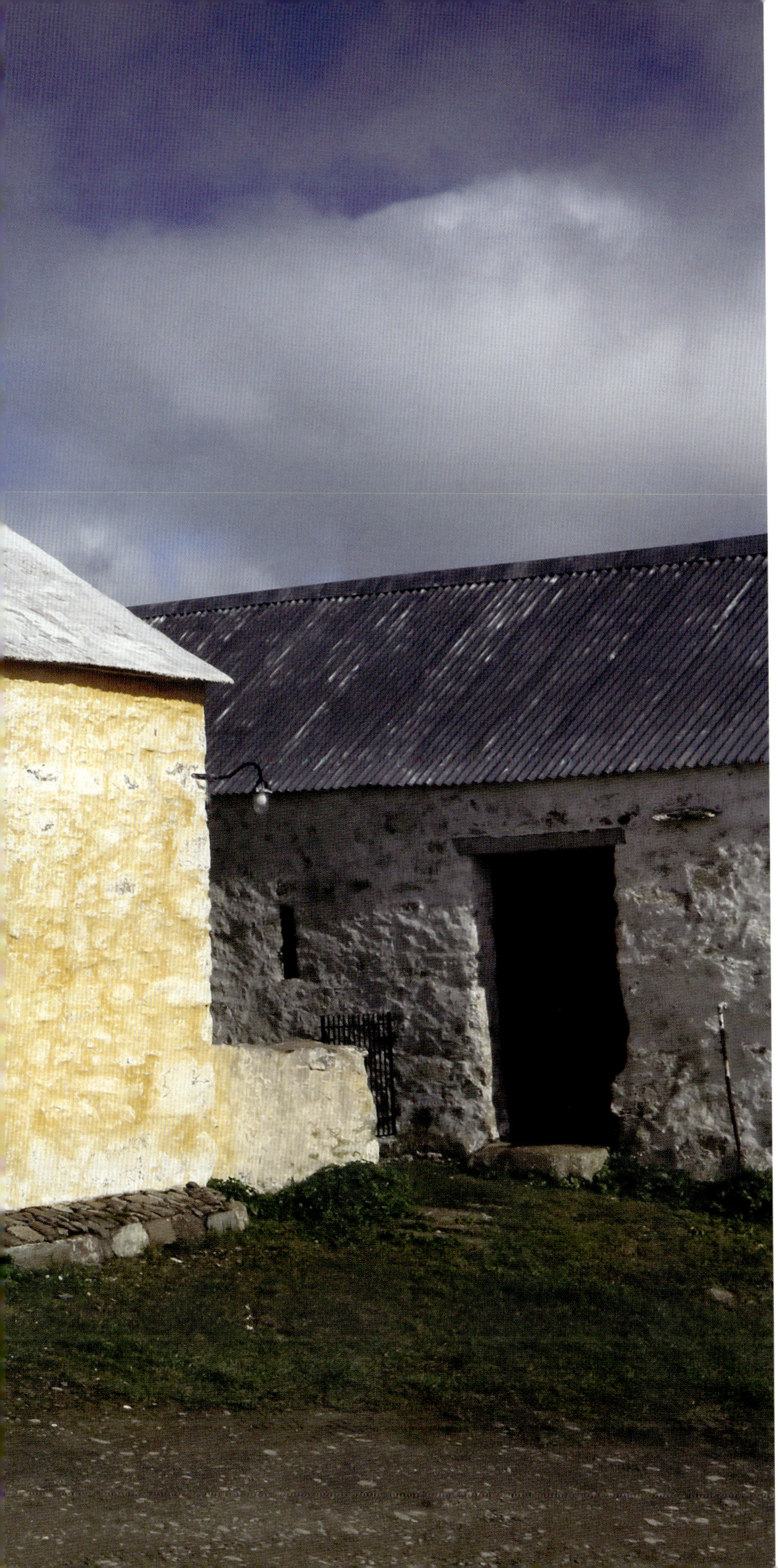

Treleddyd Fawr, Pembrokeshire, 2021.

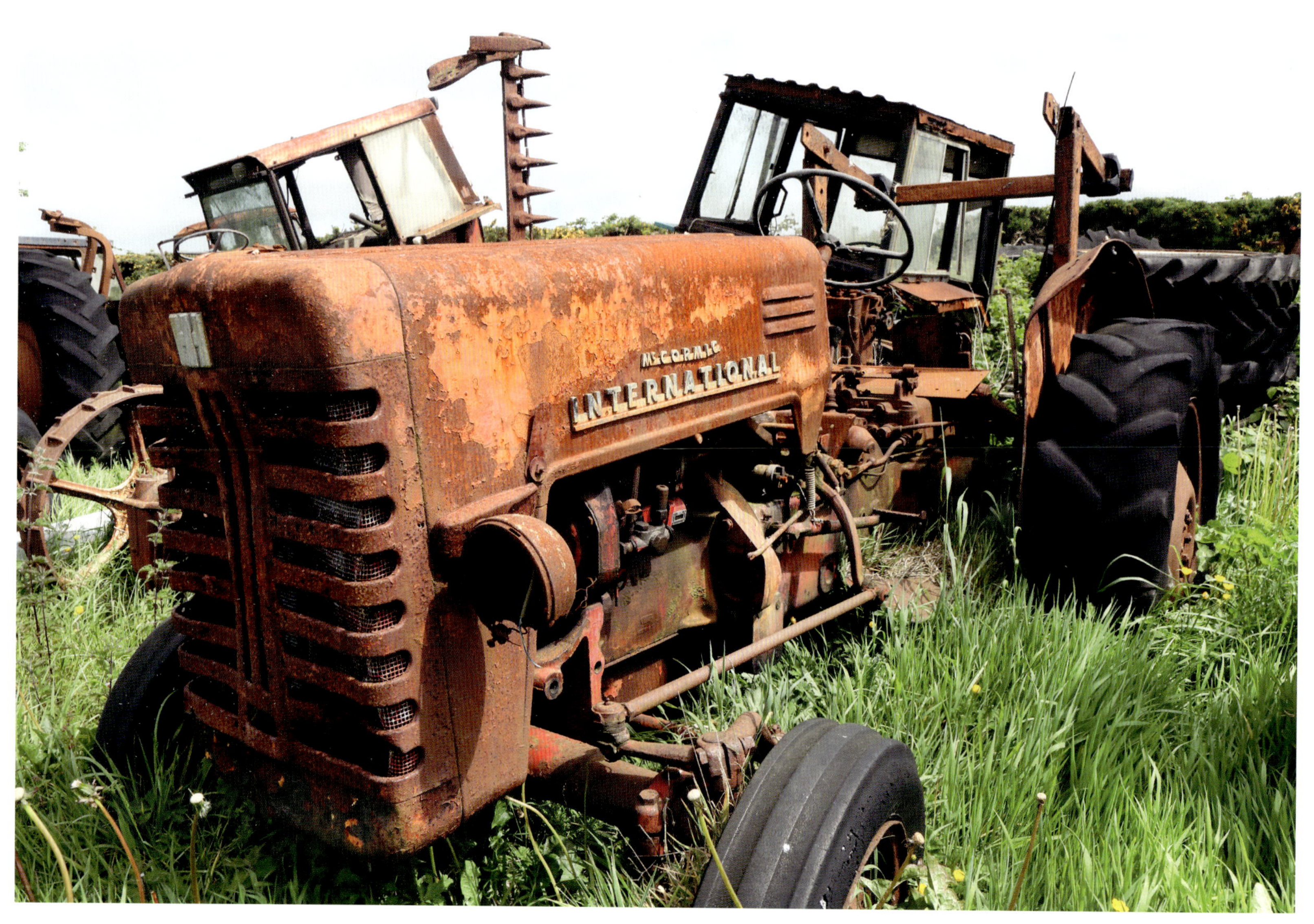

Above: Pembrokeshire, 2022.

Right: Wiston, Pembrokeshire, 2008.

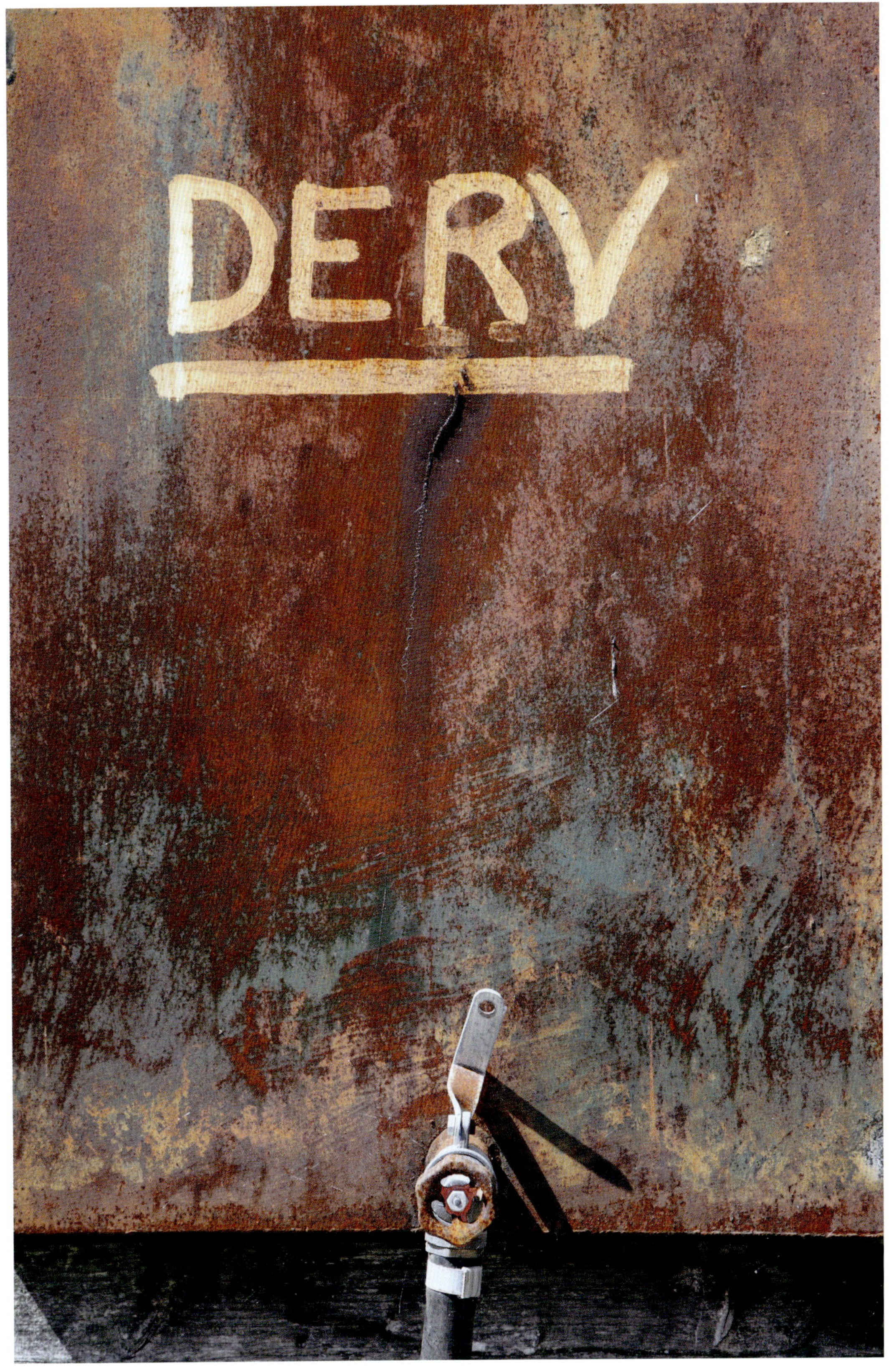
DERV

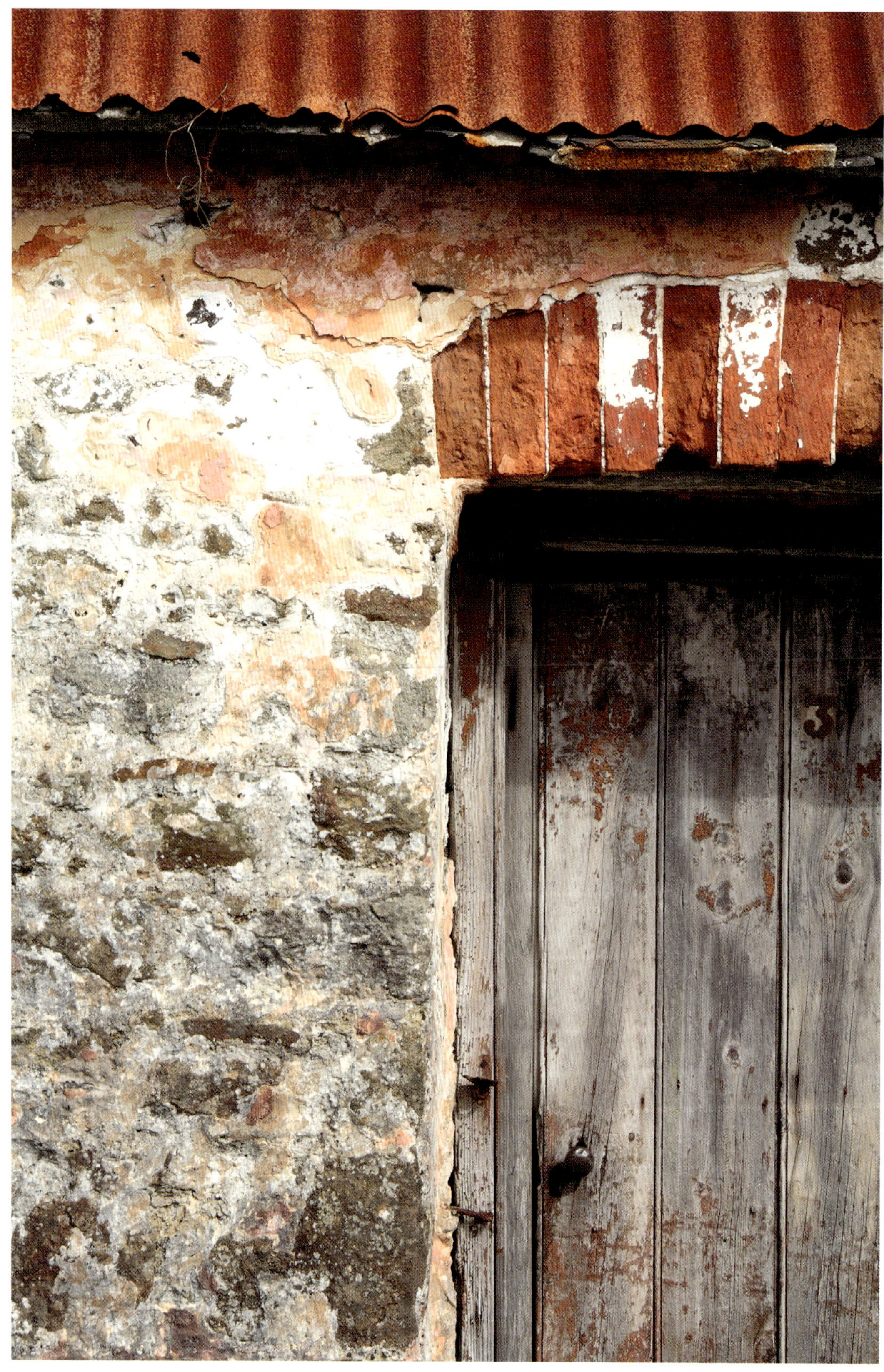

Left: Robeston Wathen,
Pembrokeshire, 2006.

Right: Pembrokeshire, 2022.

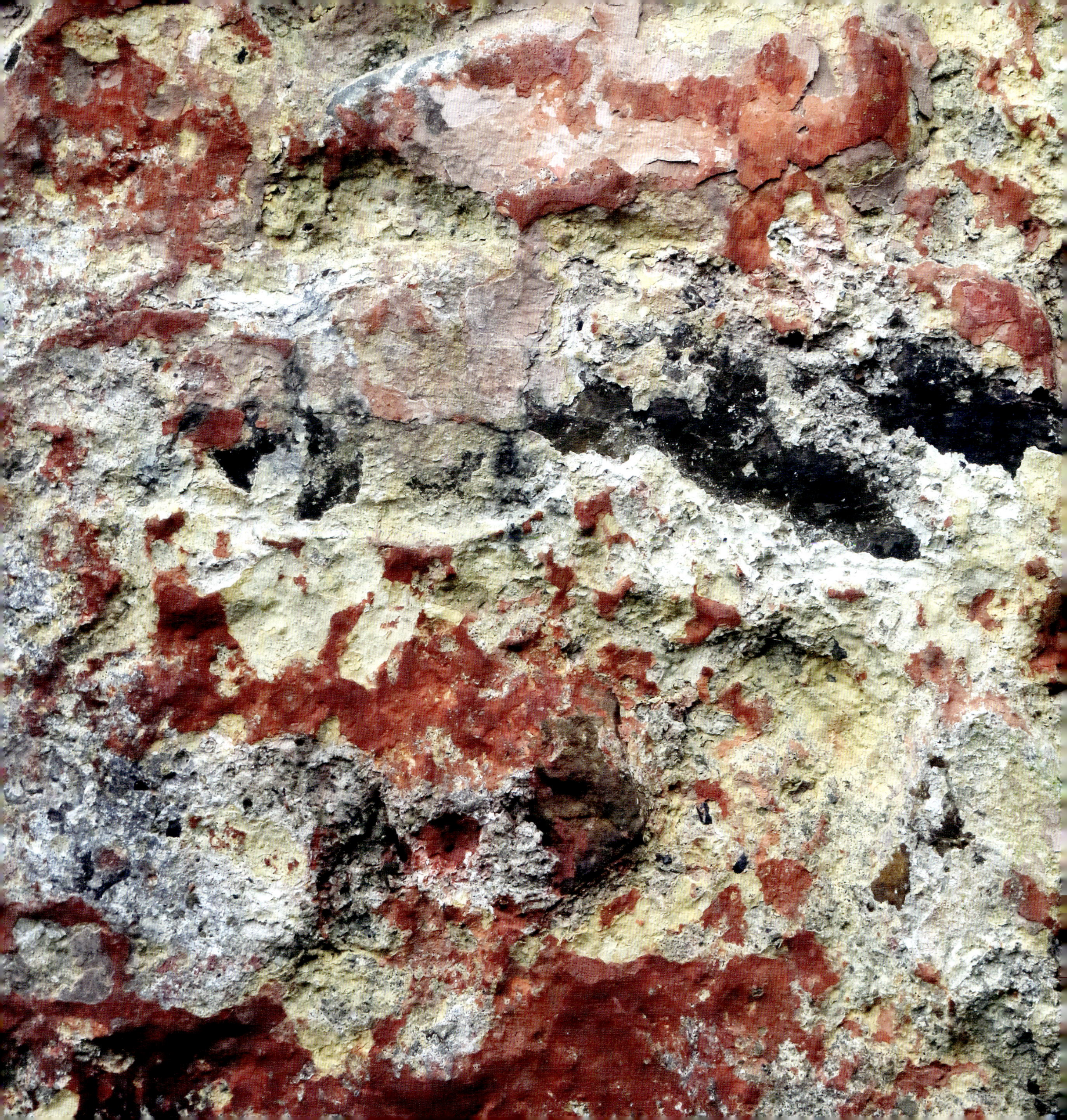

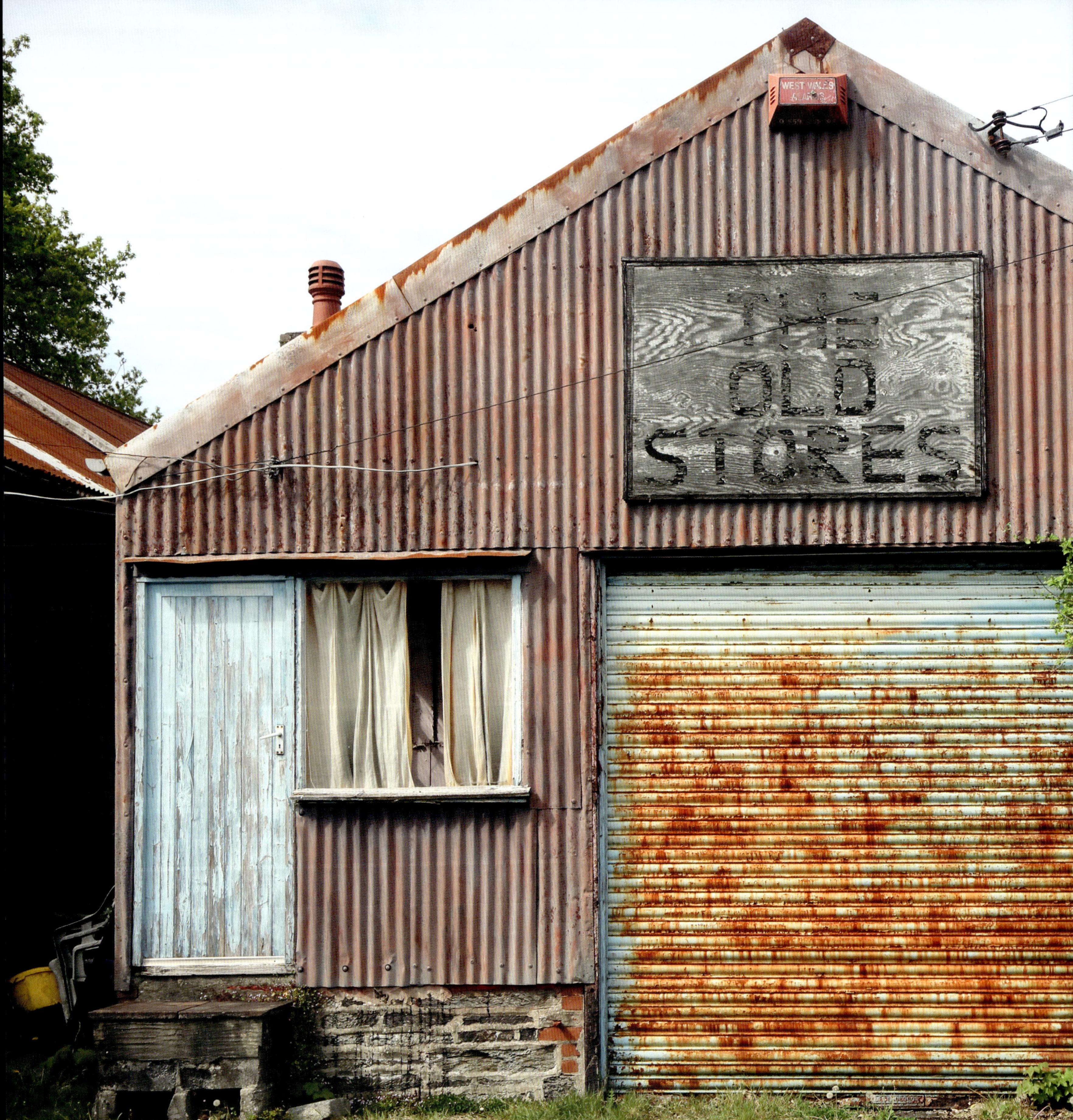

WEST WALES
ALARMS
THE
OLD
STORES

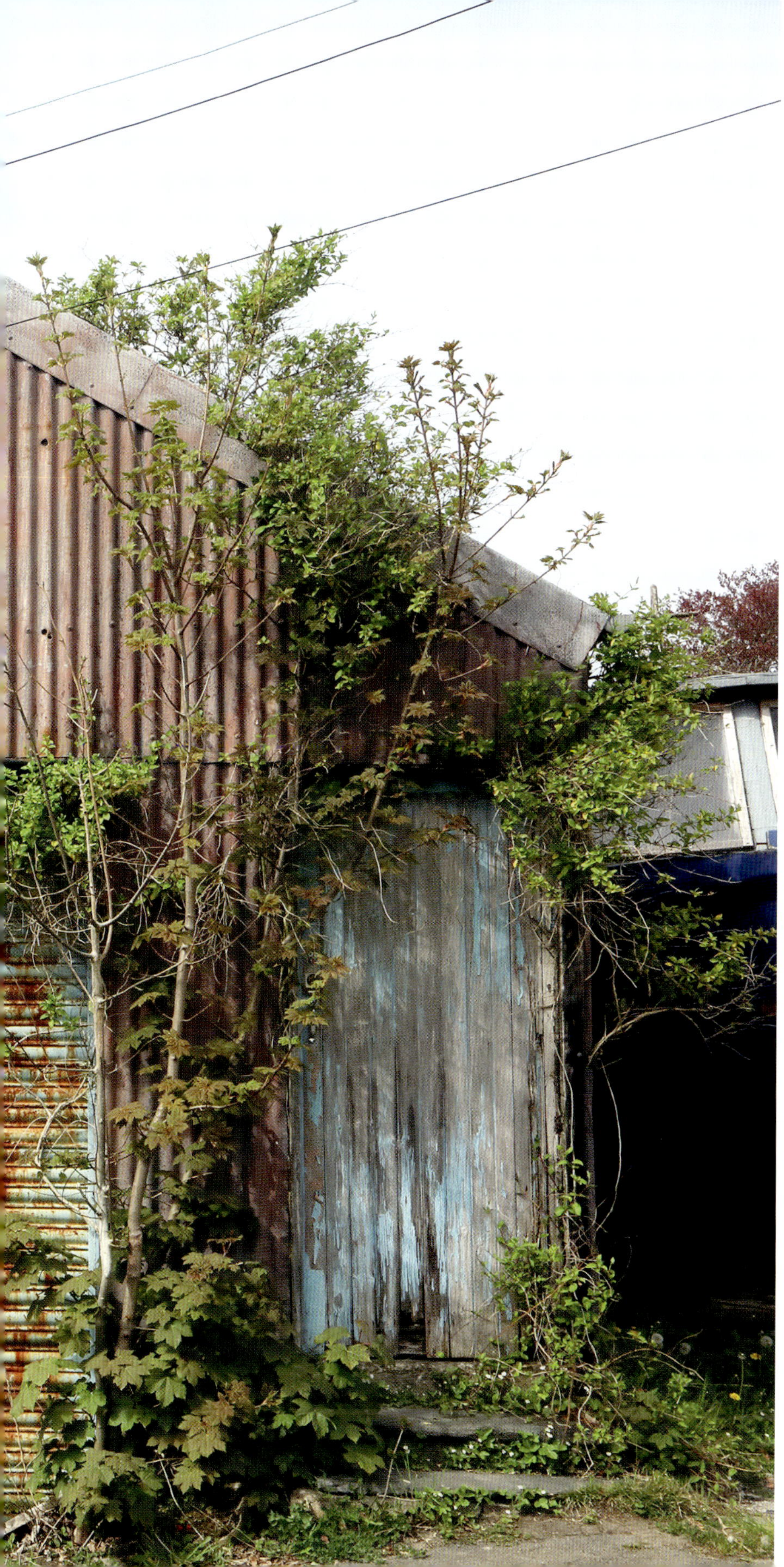

Henllan, Ceredigion, 2022.

Page 36: Llanrhian, Pembrokeshire, 2019.

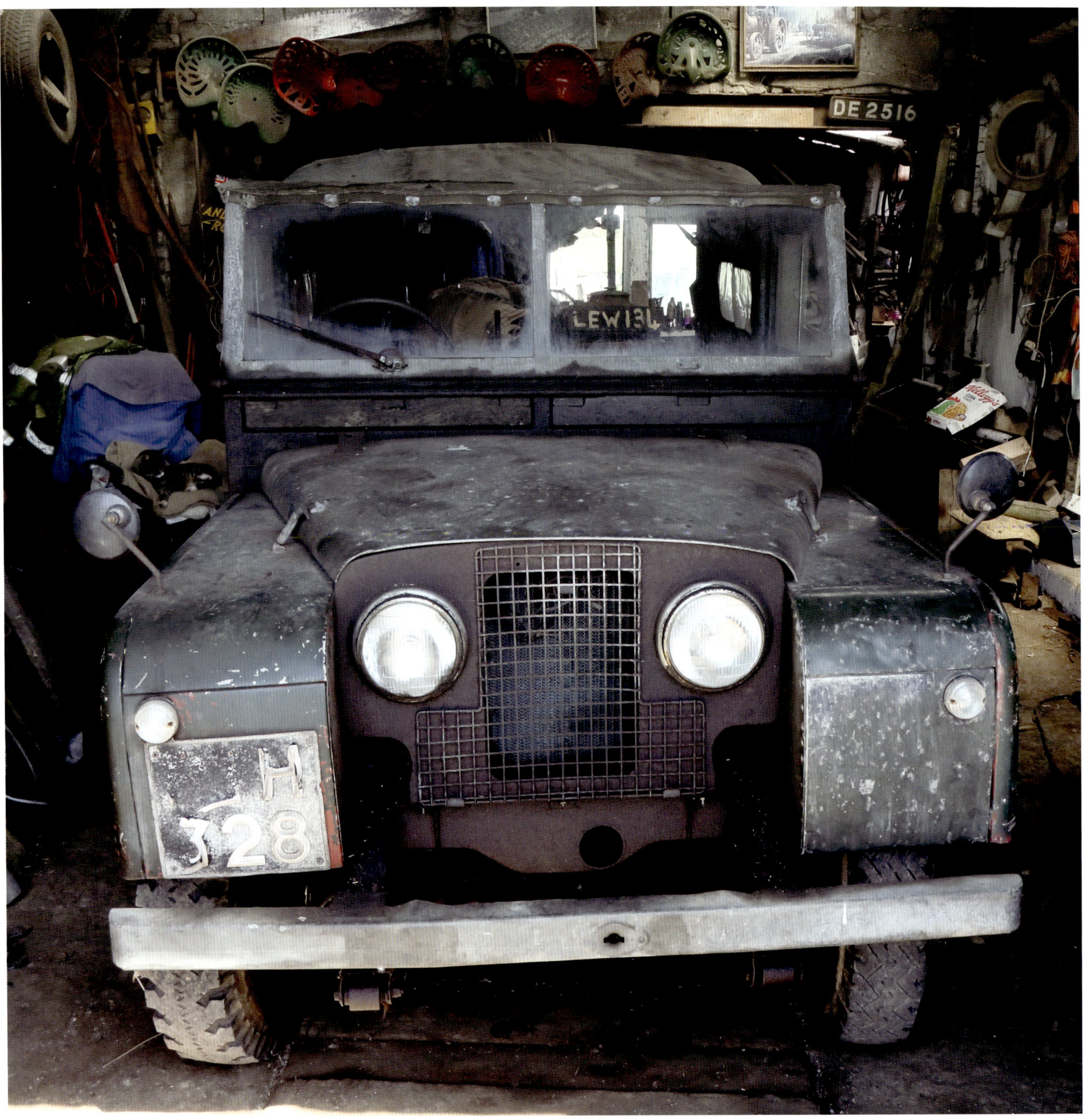
DE 2516
LEWIS

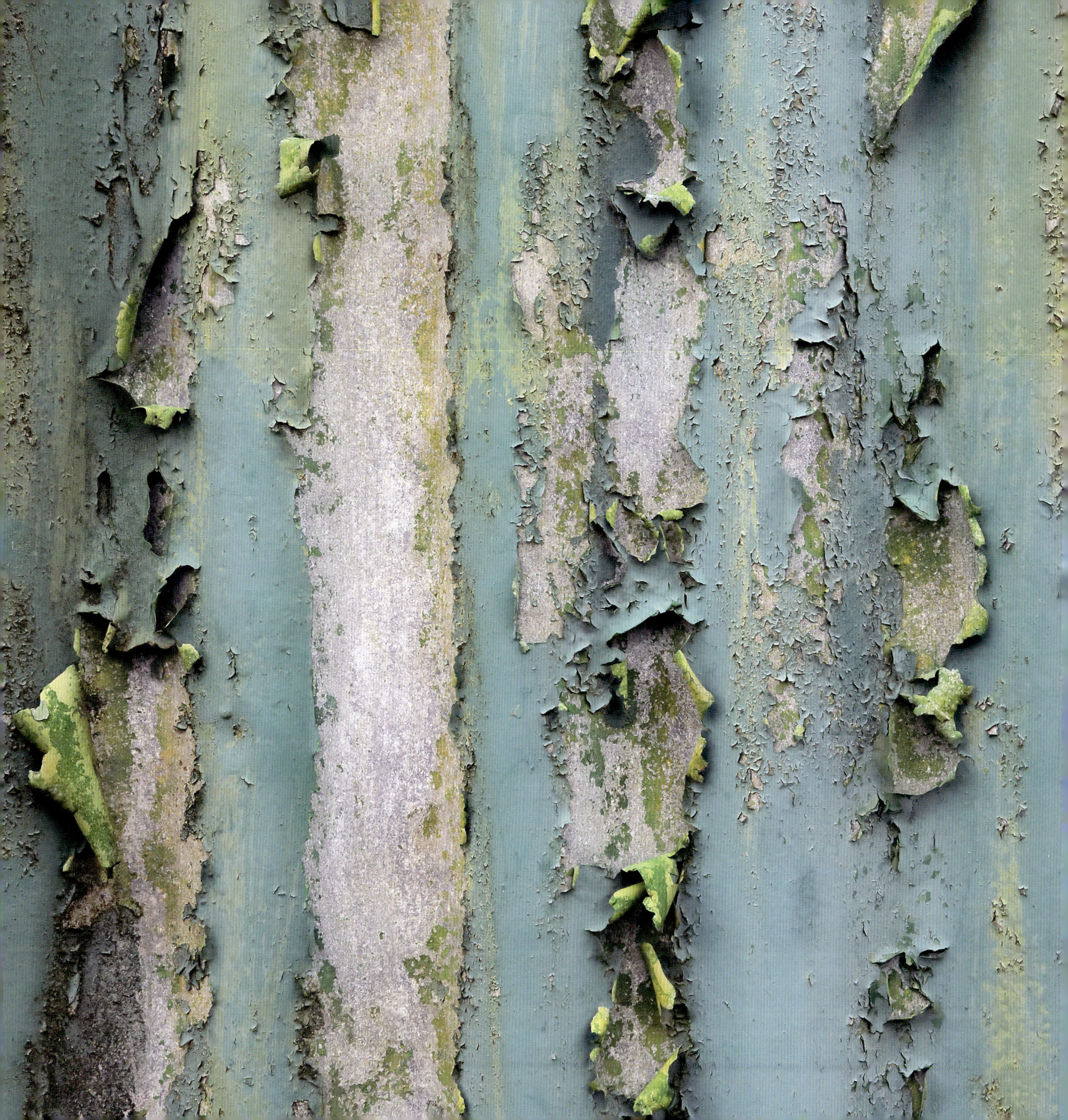

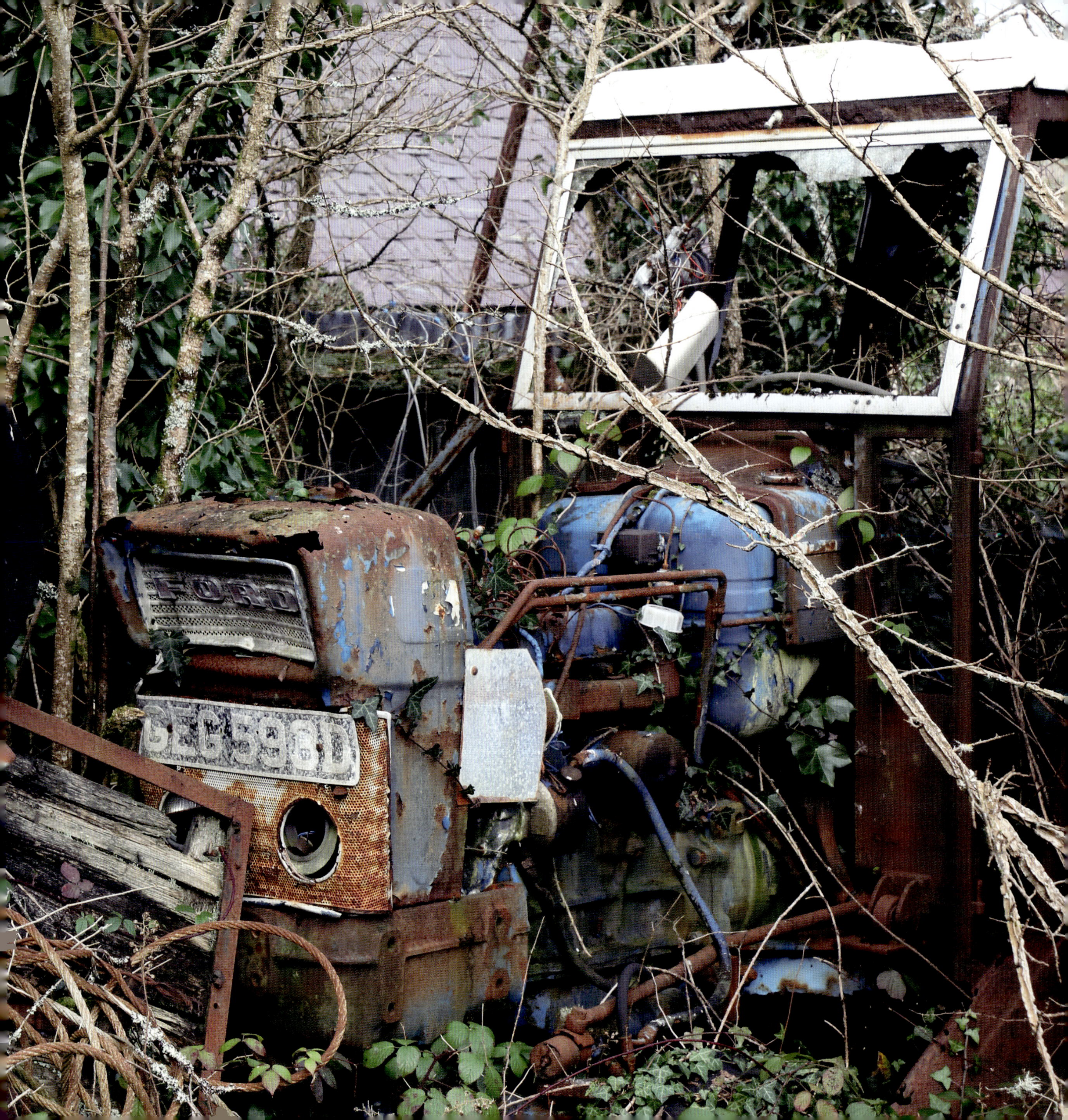
FORD
GEC596D

Left: Landshipping,
Pembrokeshire, 2022.

Right: Laugharne,
Carmarthenshire, 2006.

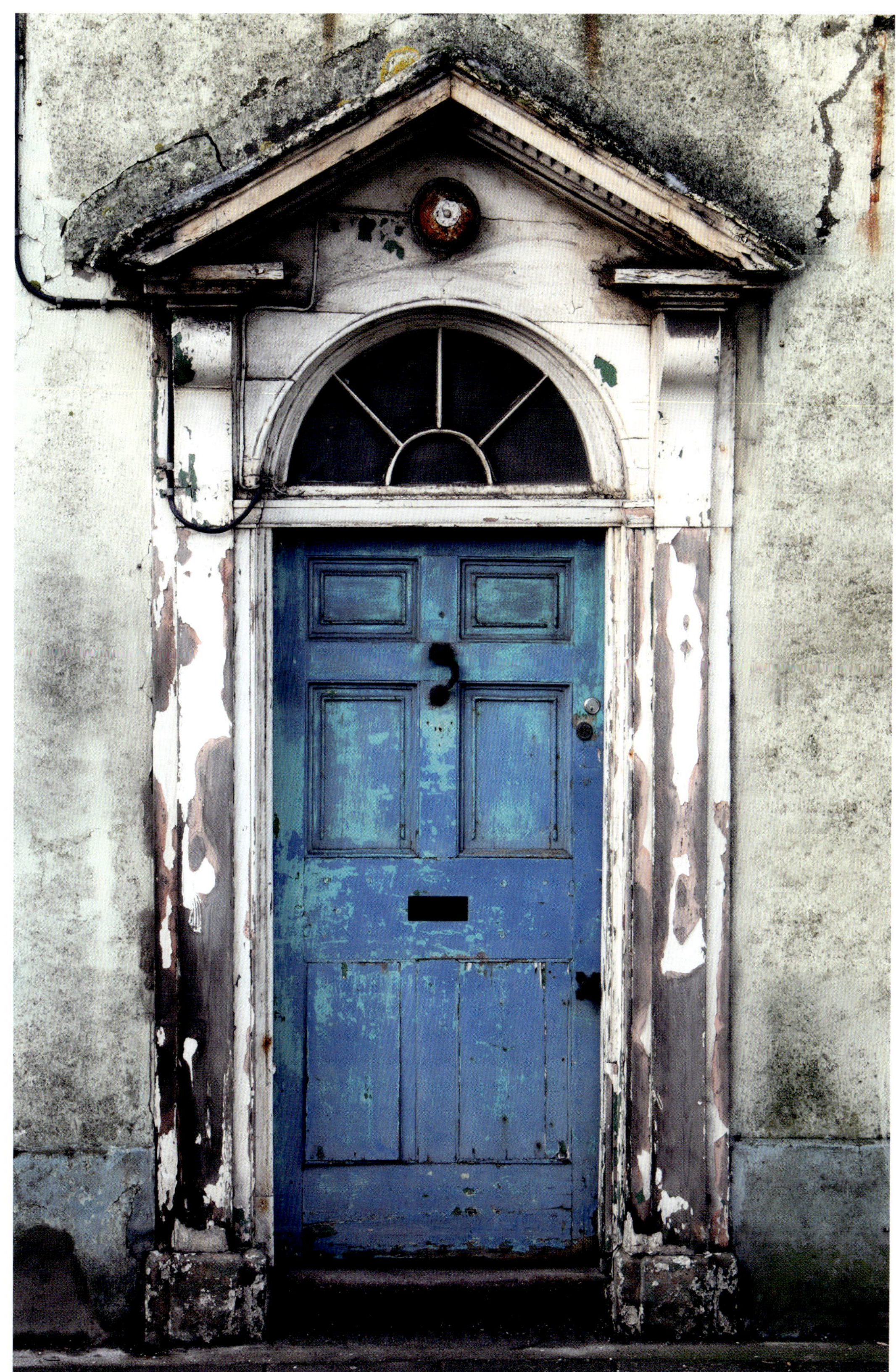

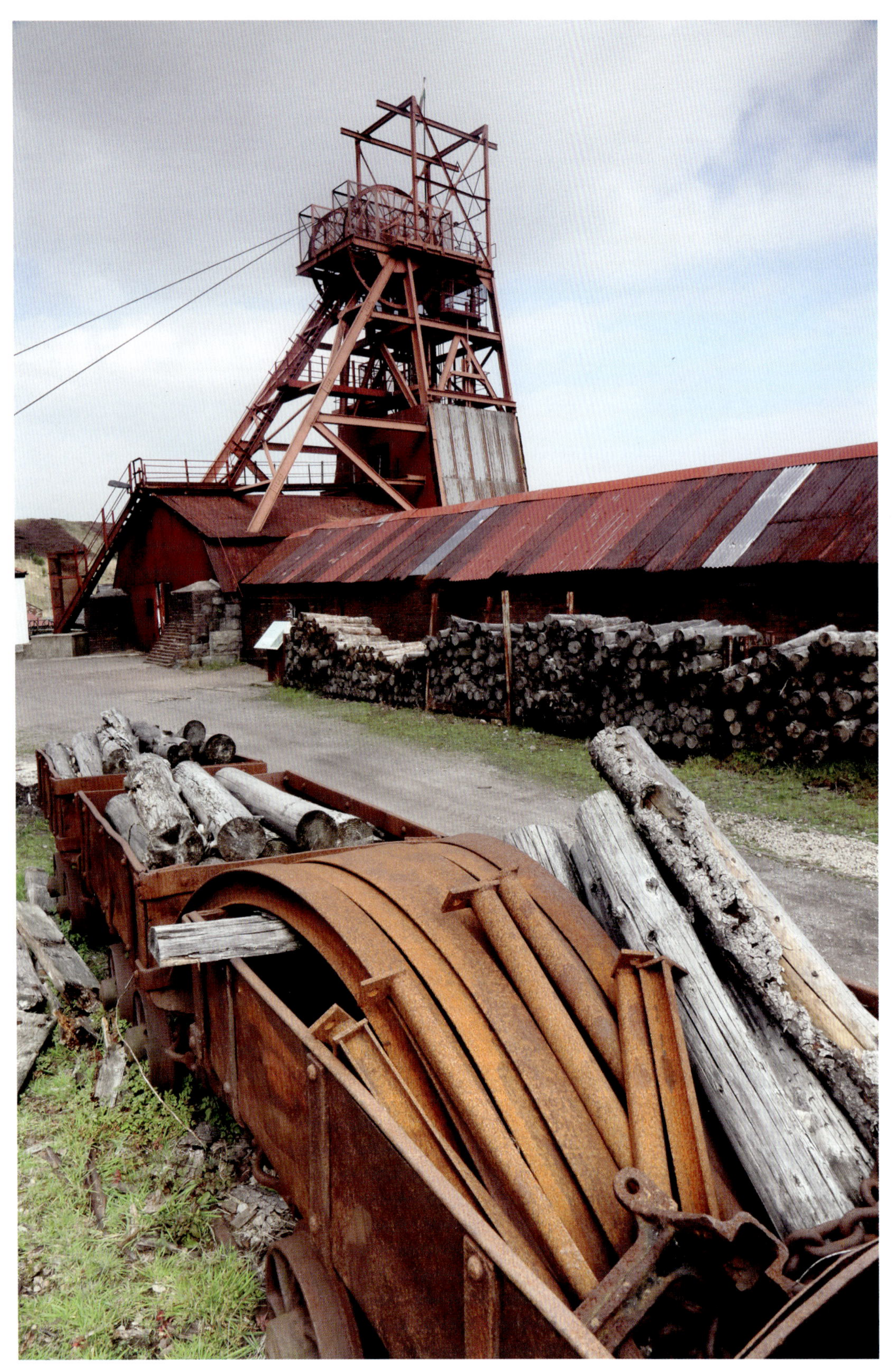

Left: Big Pit, Blaenavon, Gwent, 2014.

Right: Cresswell Quay, Pembrokeshire, 2022.

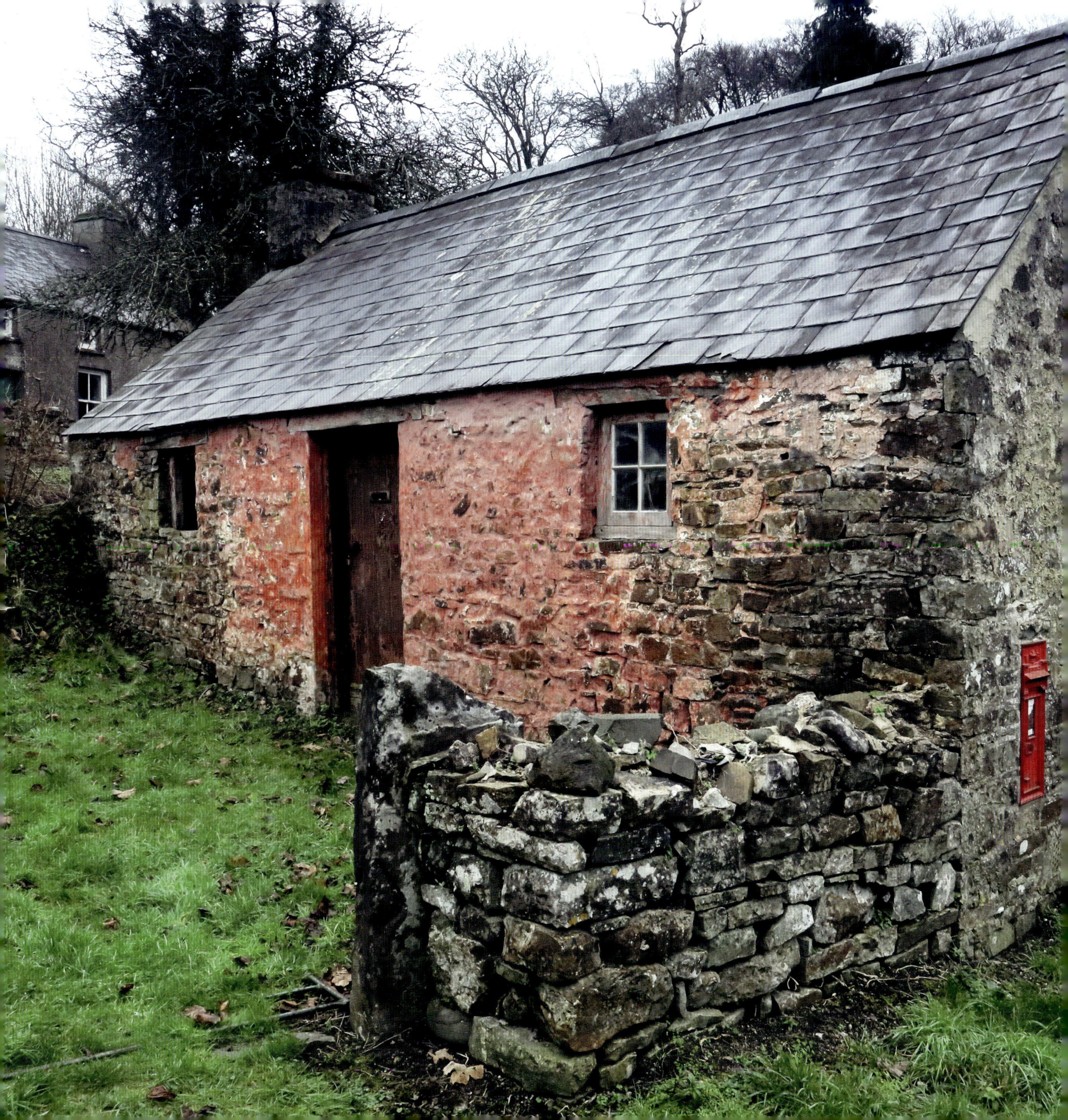

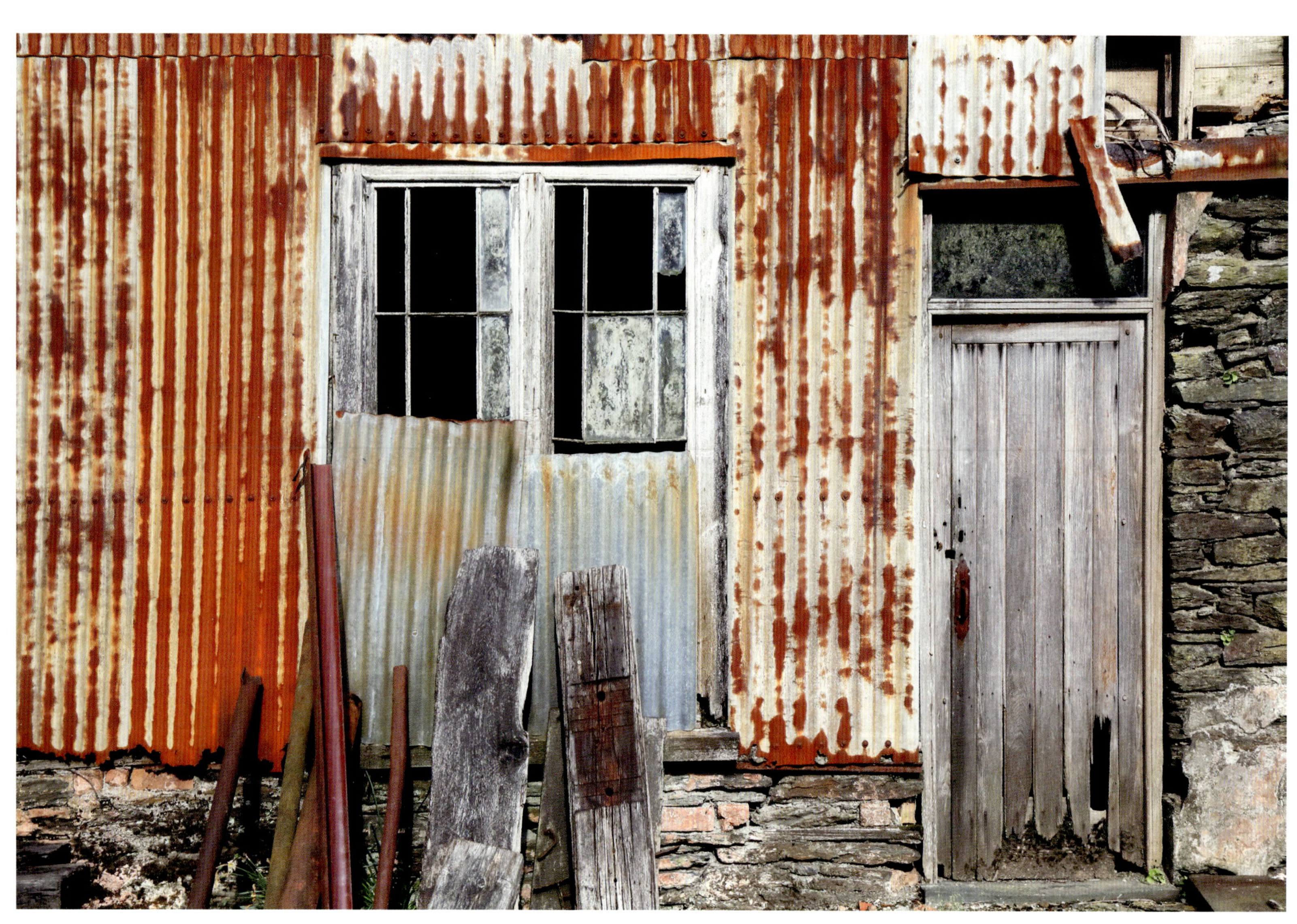

Dinas, Carmarthenshire, 2022.

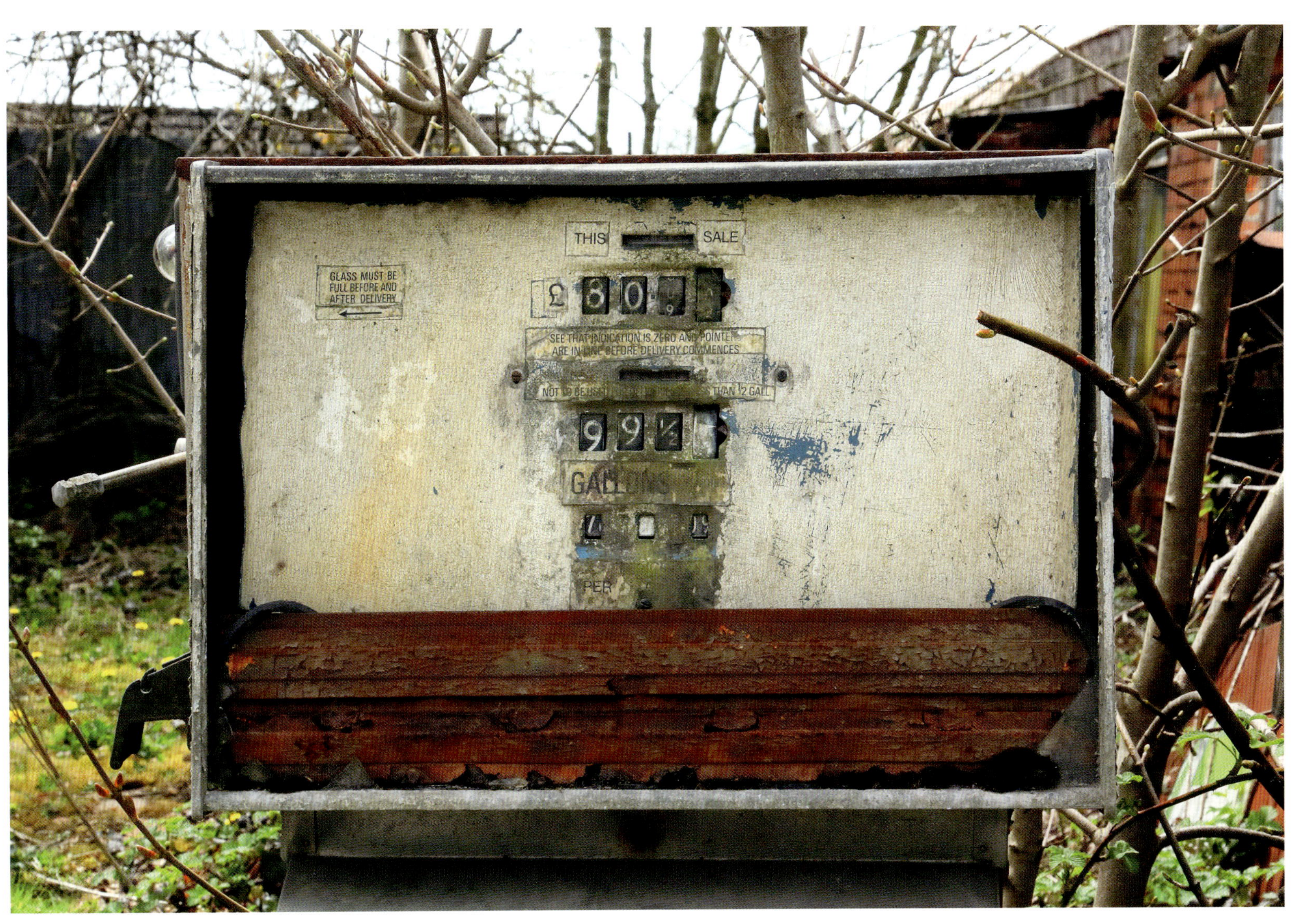

Gorsgoch, Ceredigion, 2022.

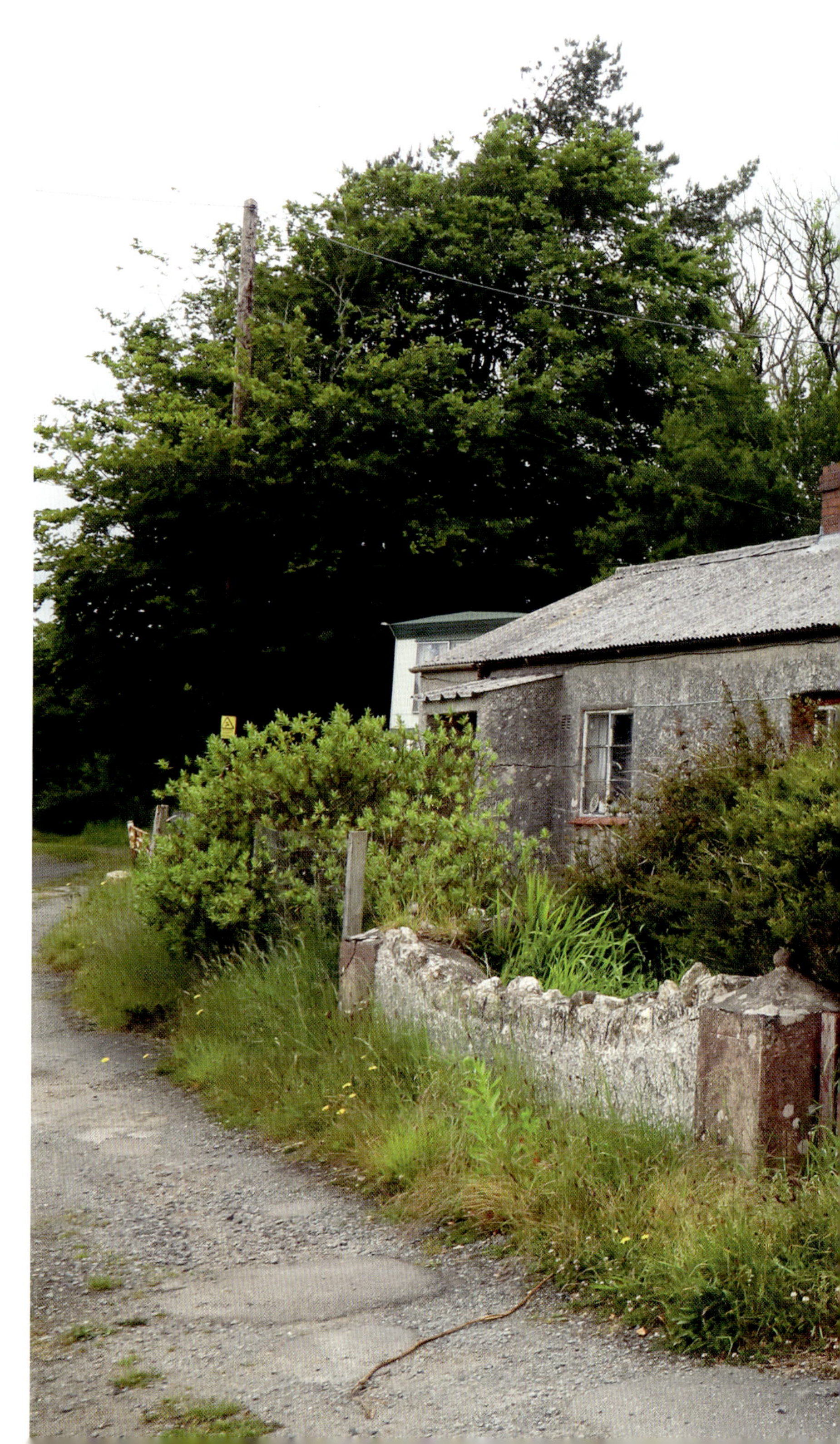

Wolfscastle, Pembrokeshire, 2022.

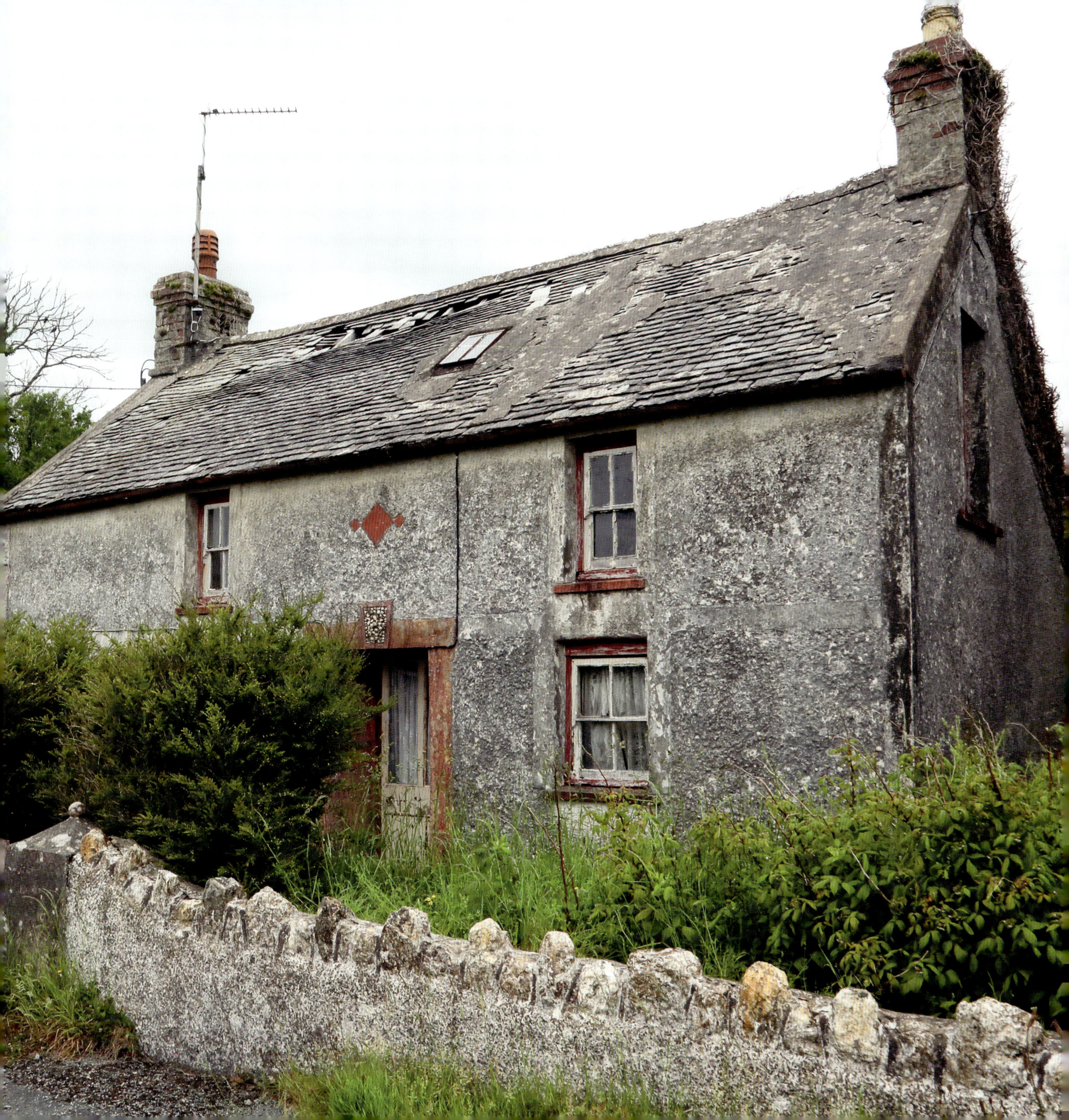

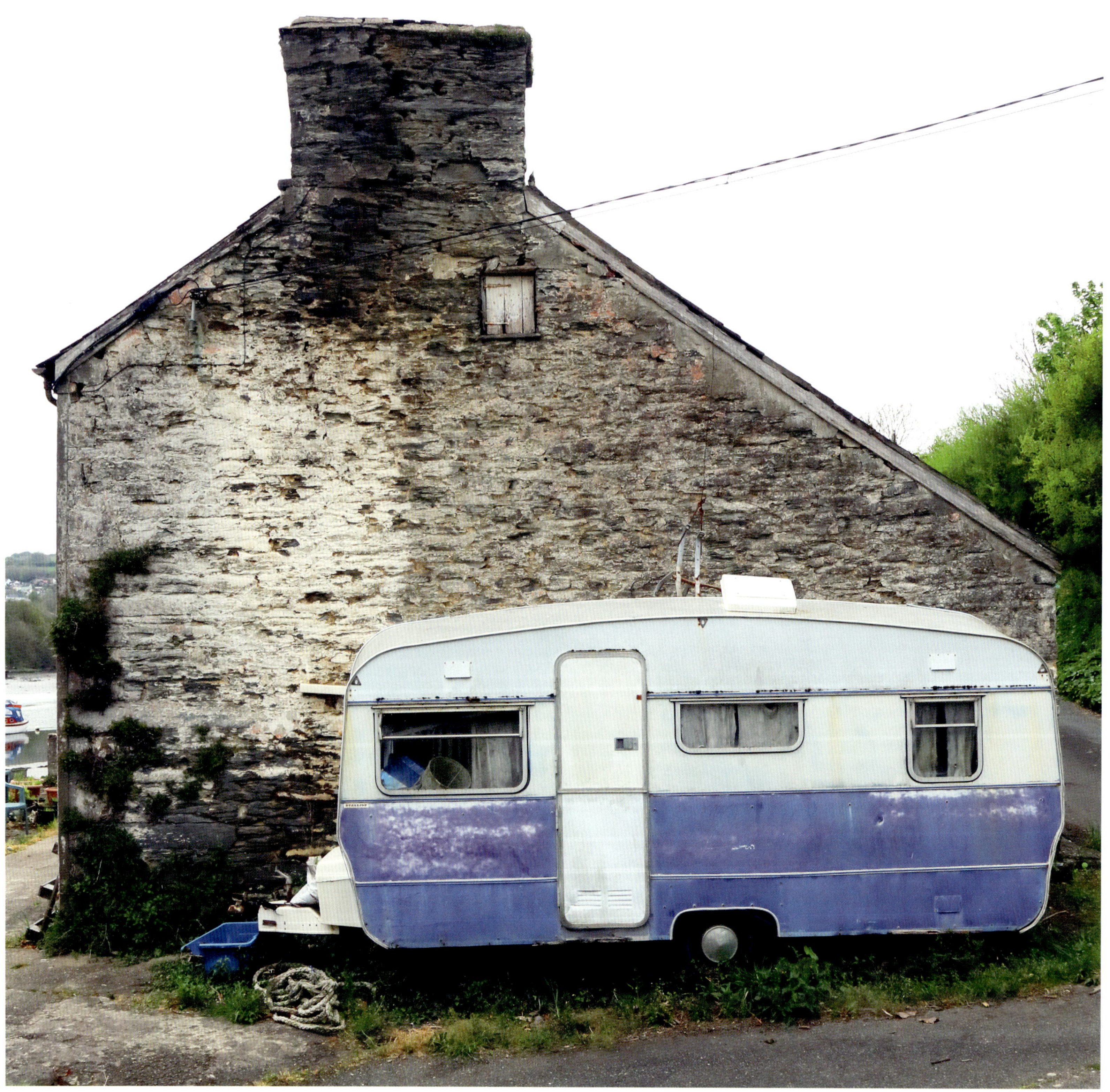

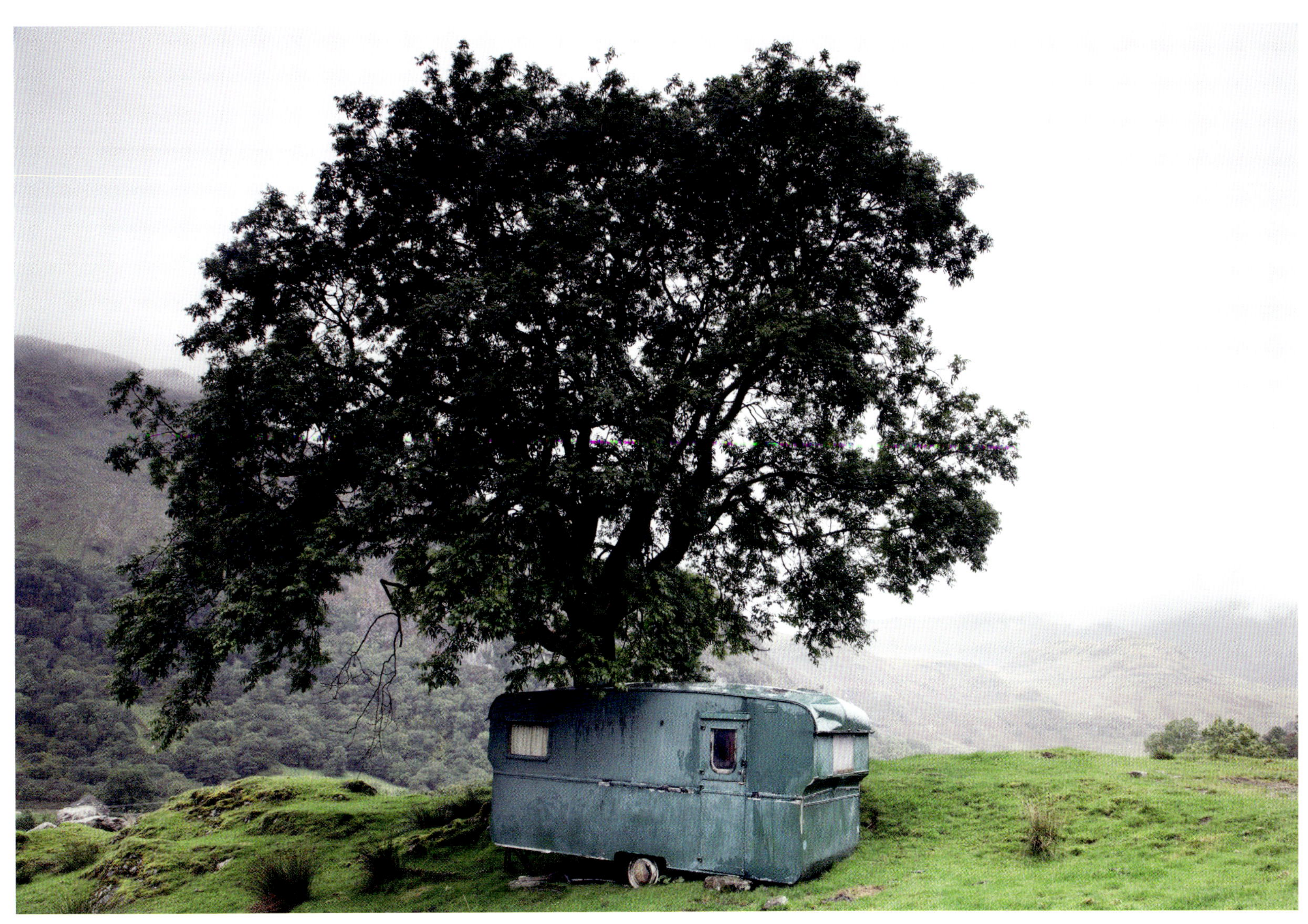

Left: Ceredigion, 2022.

Above: Nant Gwynant, Snowdonia
National Park, 2010.

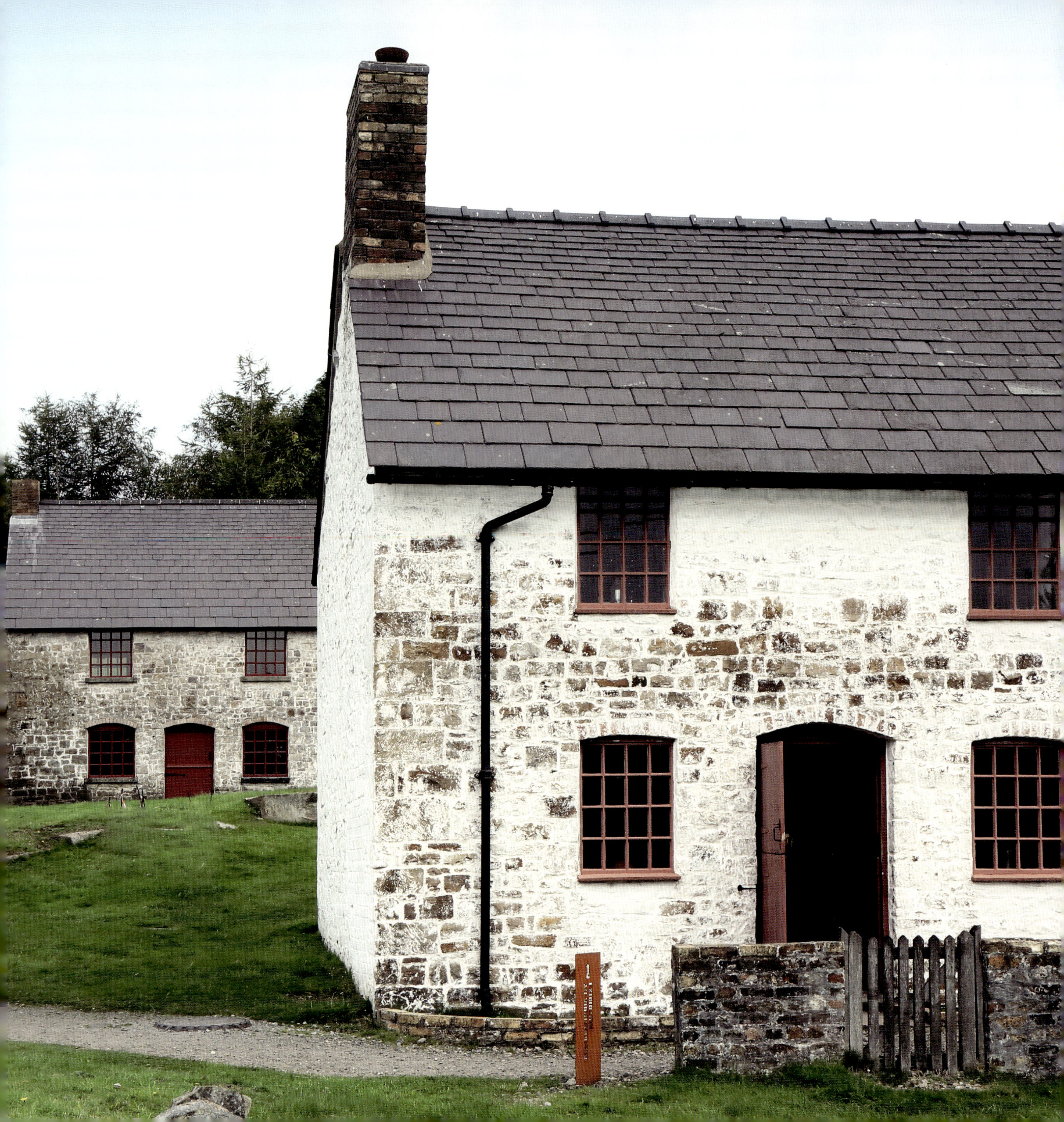

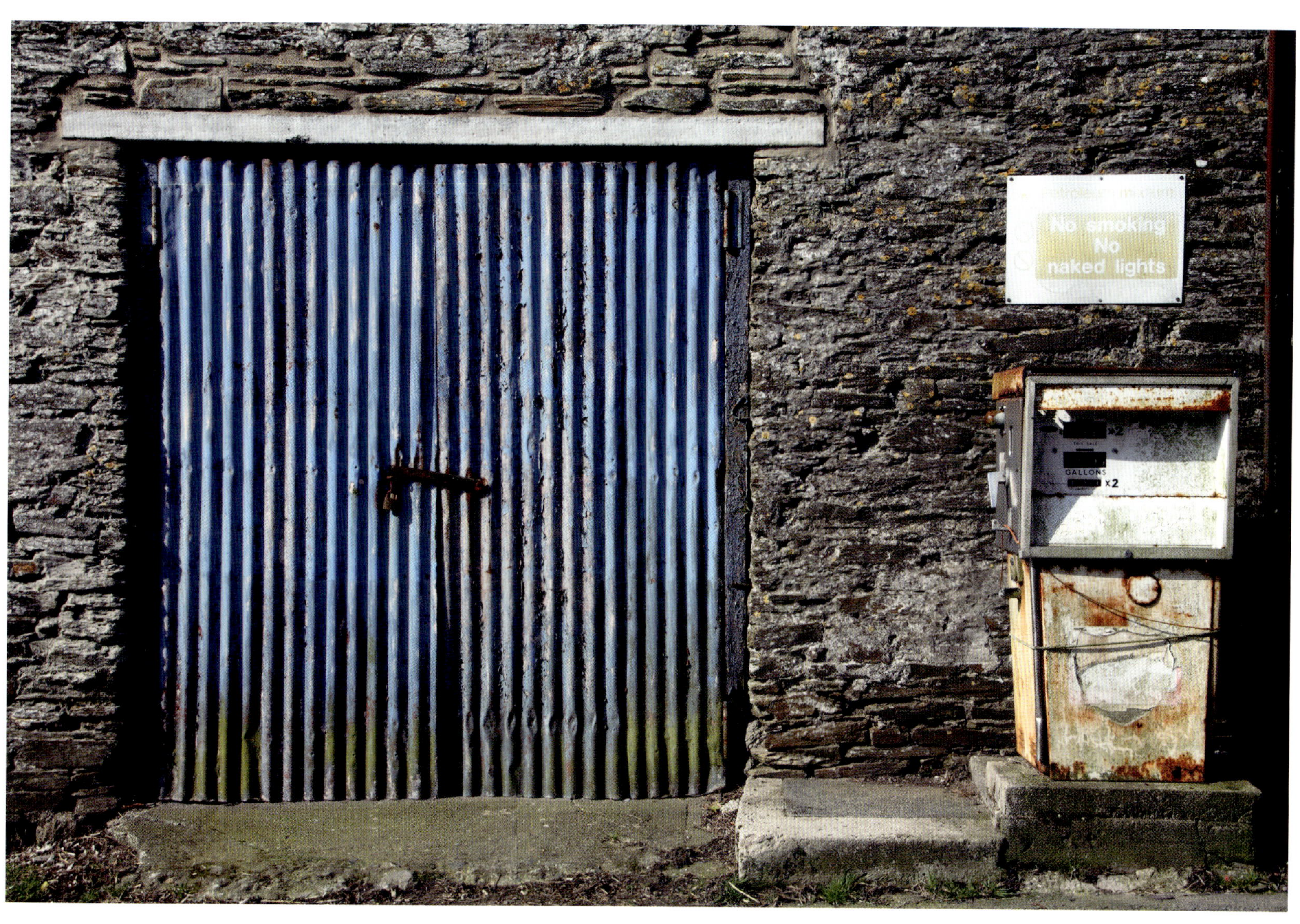

Left: Blaenavon Ironworks, Gwent, 2014.

Above: Mathry, Pembrokeshire, 2006.

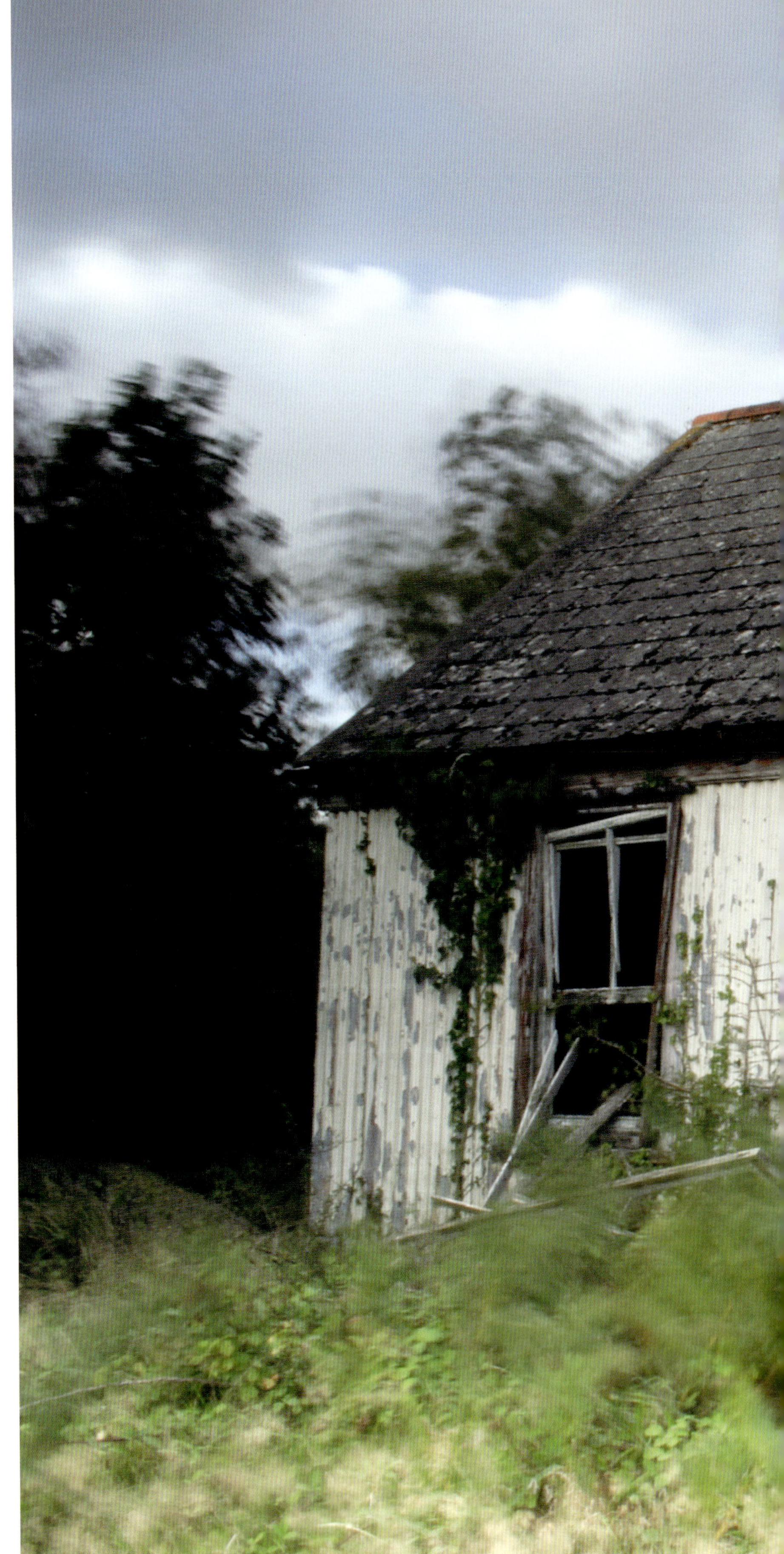

Camrose, Pembrokeshire, 2004.

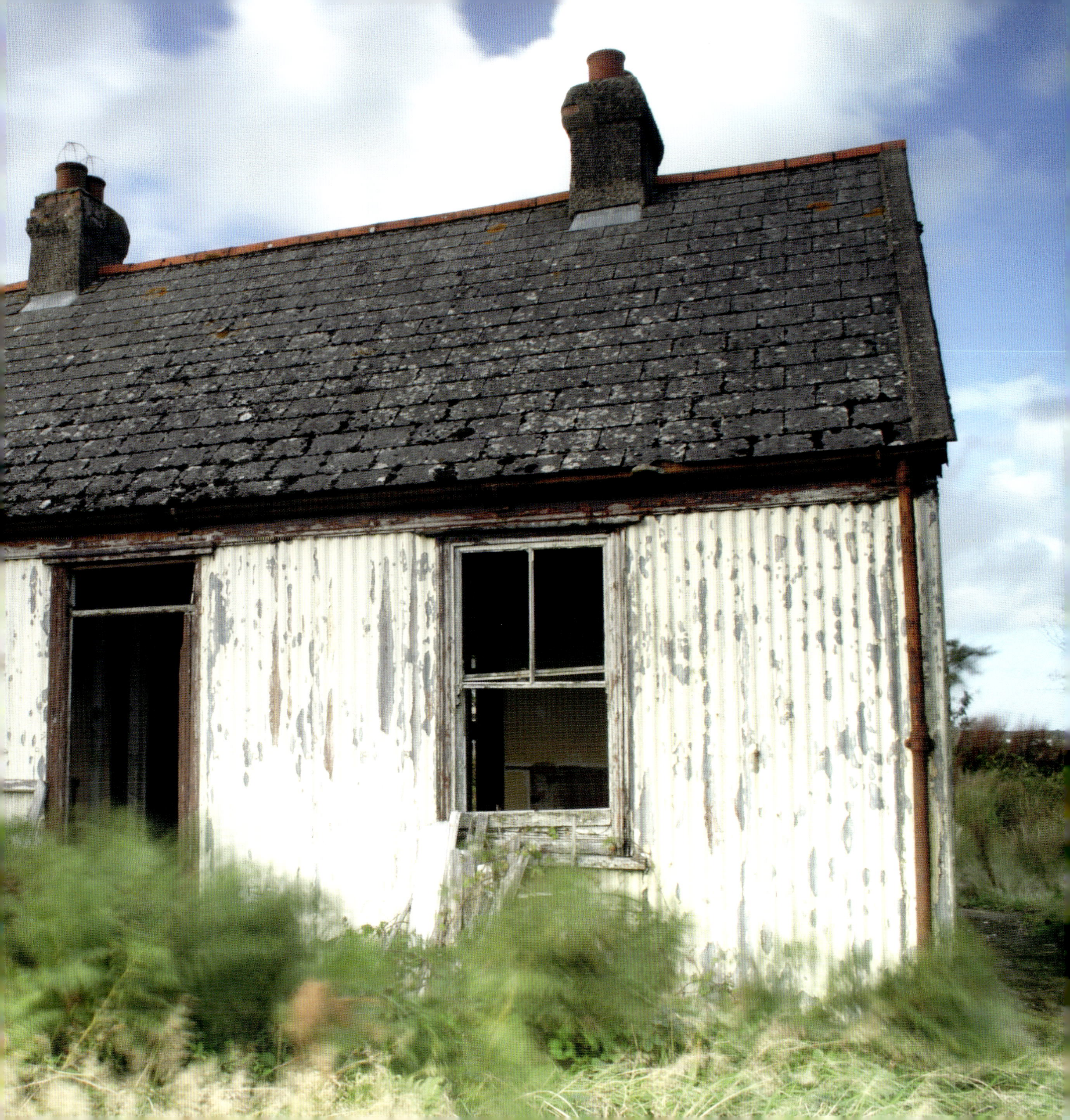

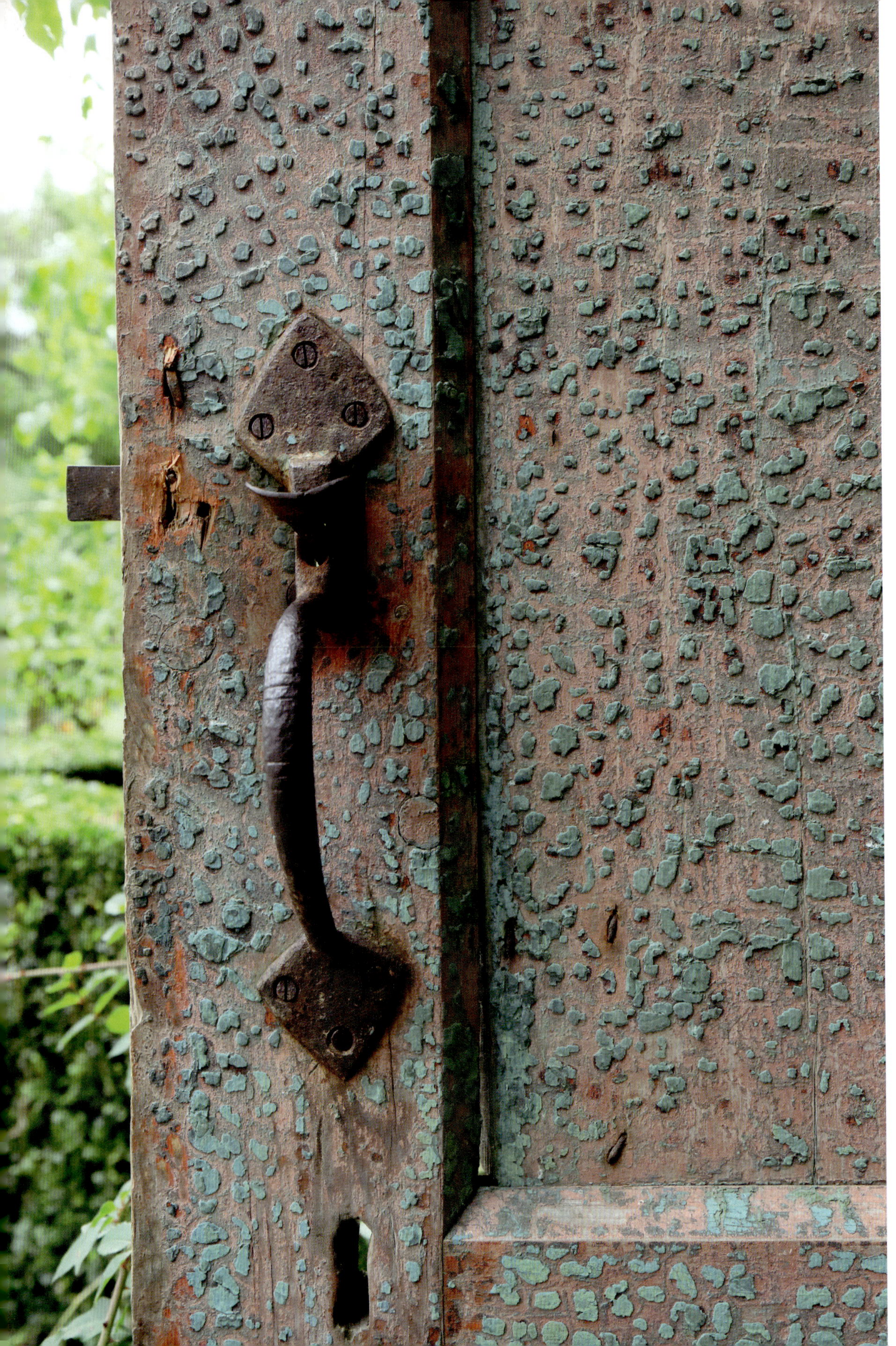

Left: Llanerchaeron,
Ceredigion, 2014.

Right: Llangwm,
Pembrokeshire, 2019.

Pages 54-55:
Llangwm,
Pembrokeshire, 2018.

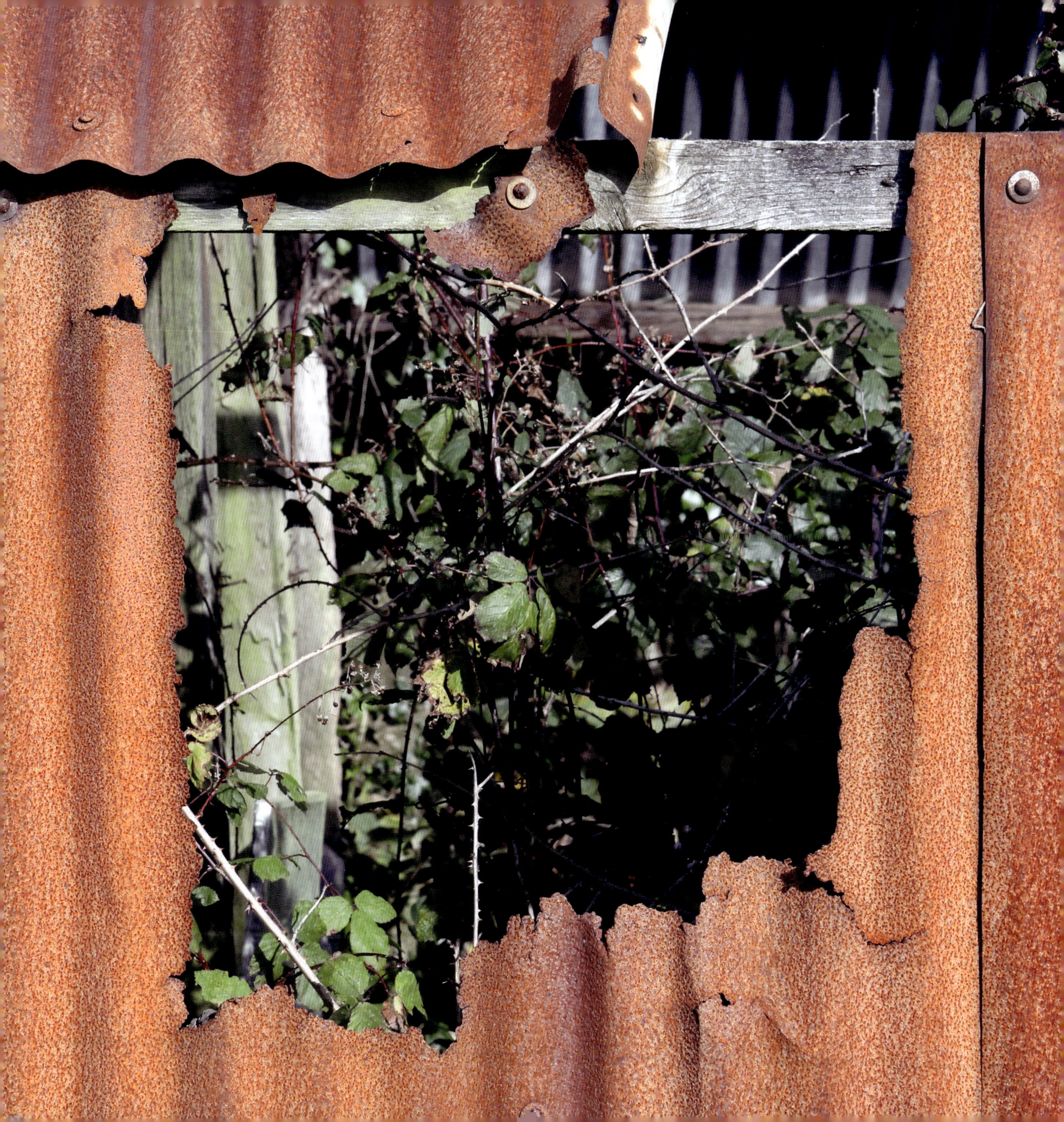

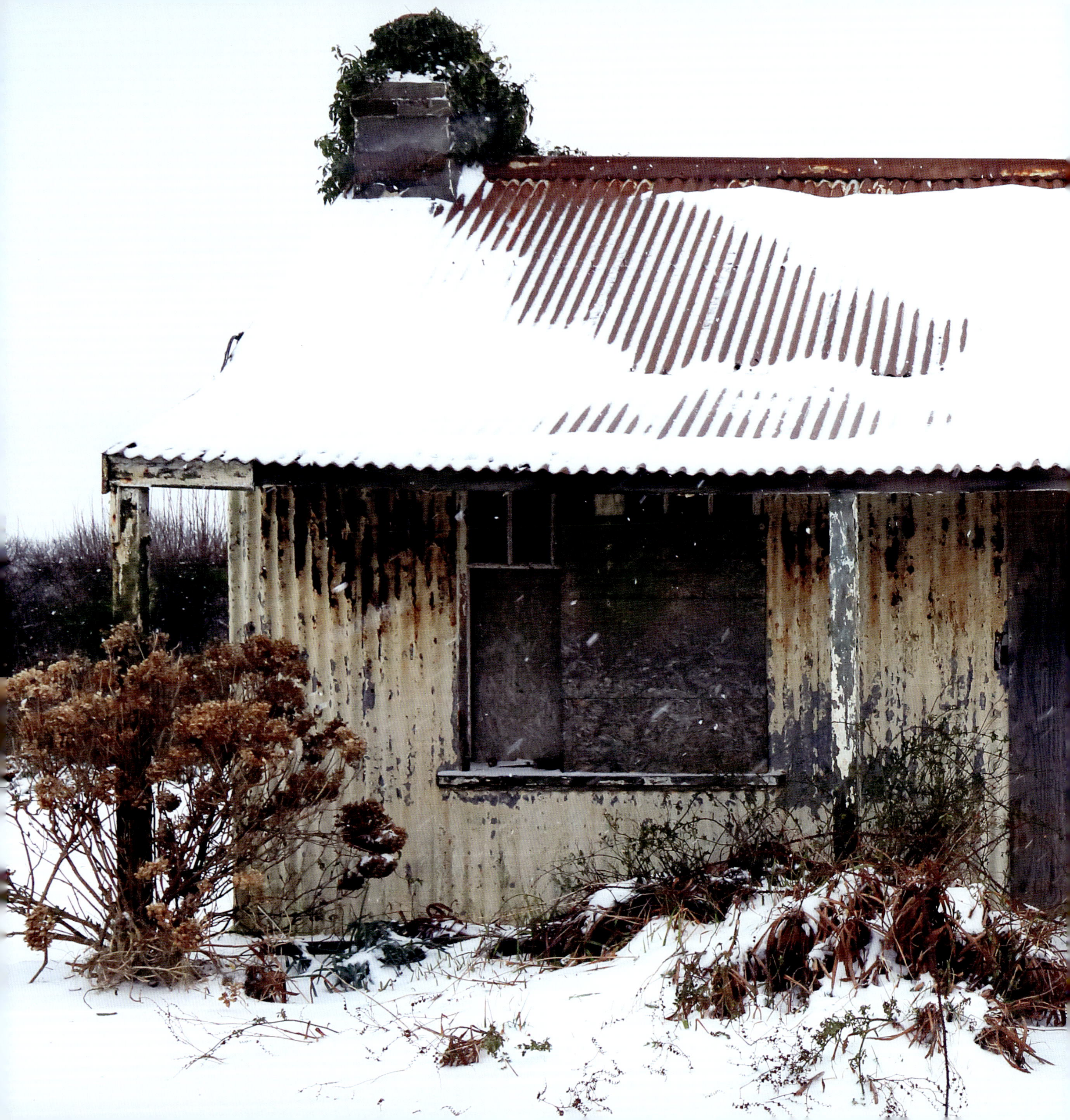

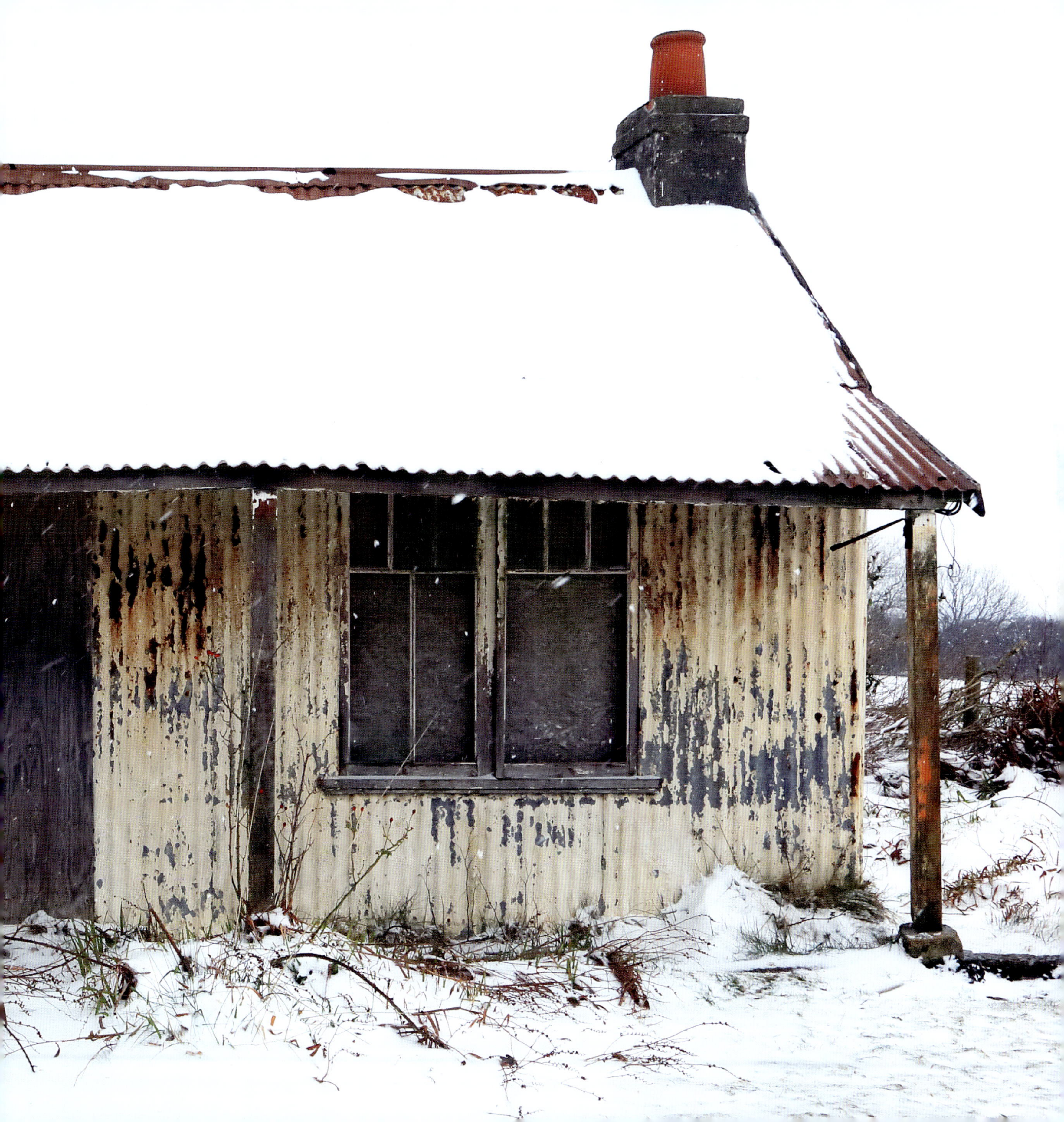

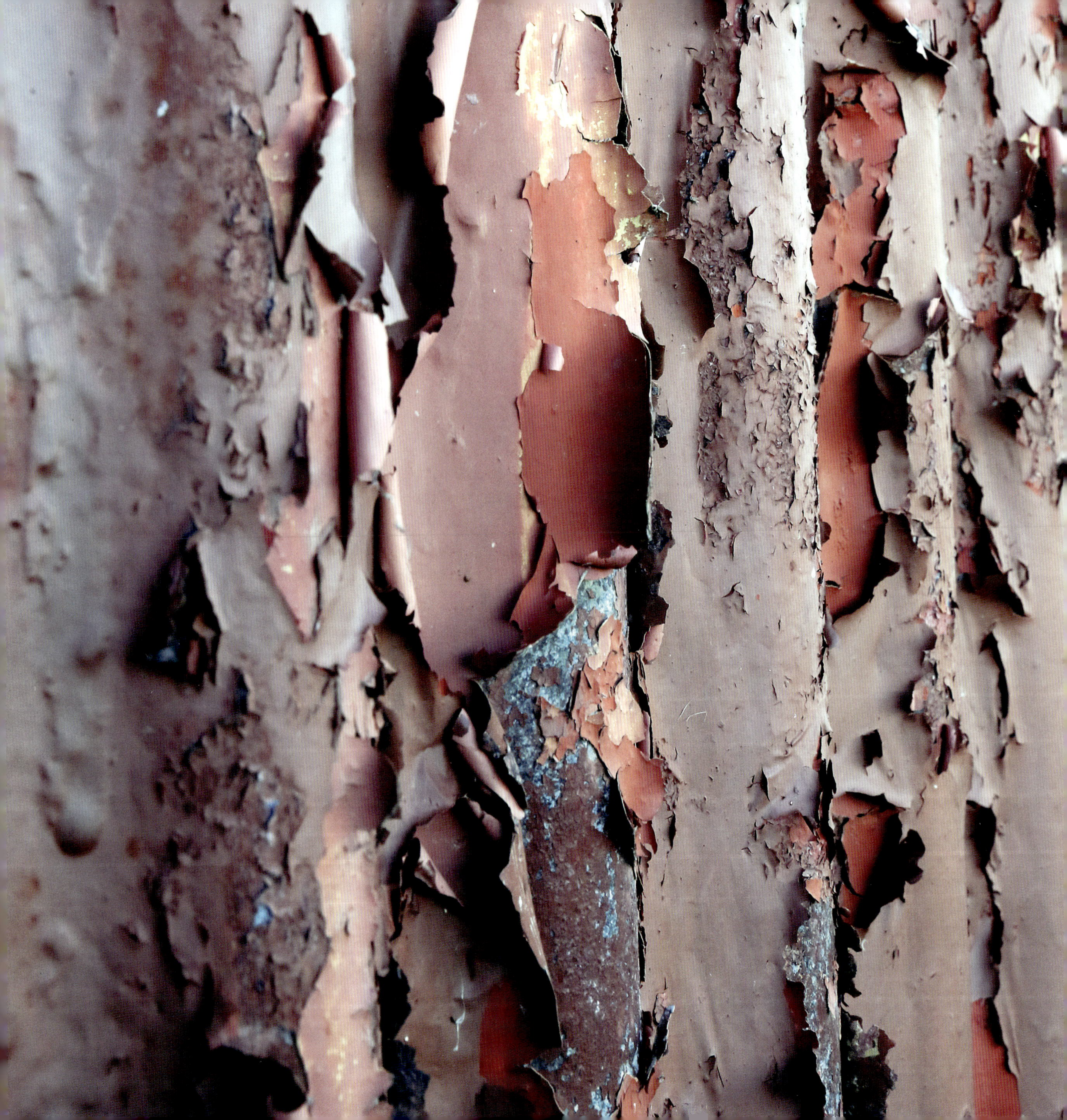

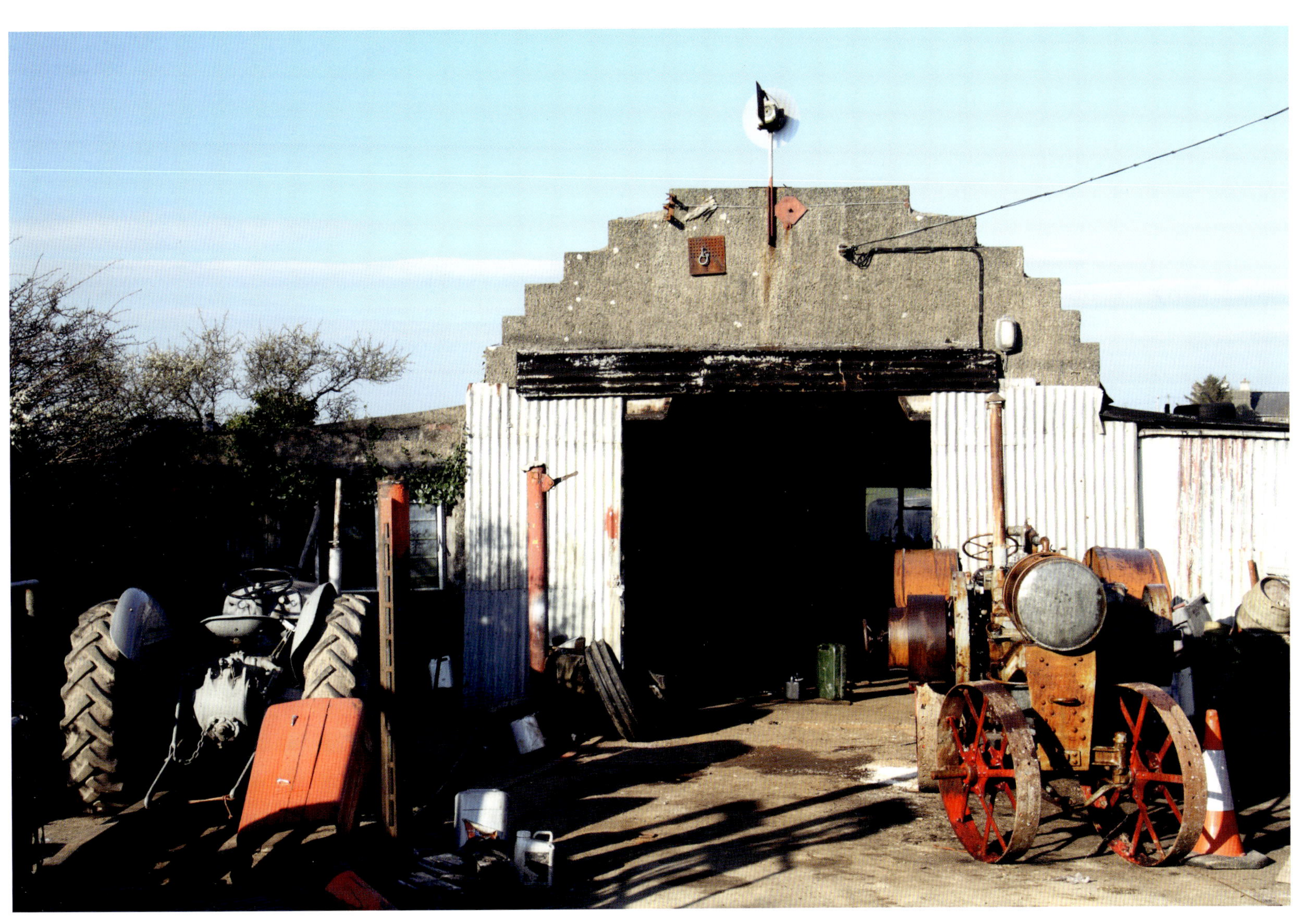

Llanrhian, Pembrokeshire, 2008.

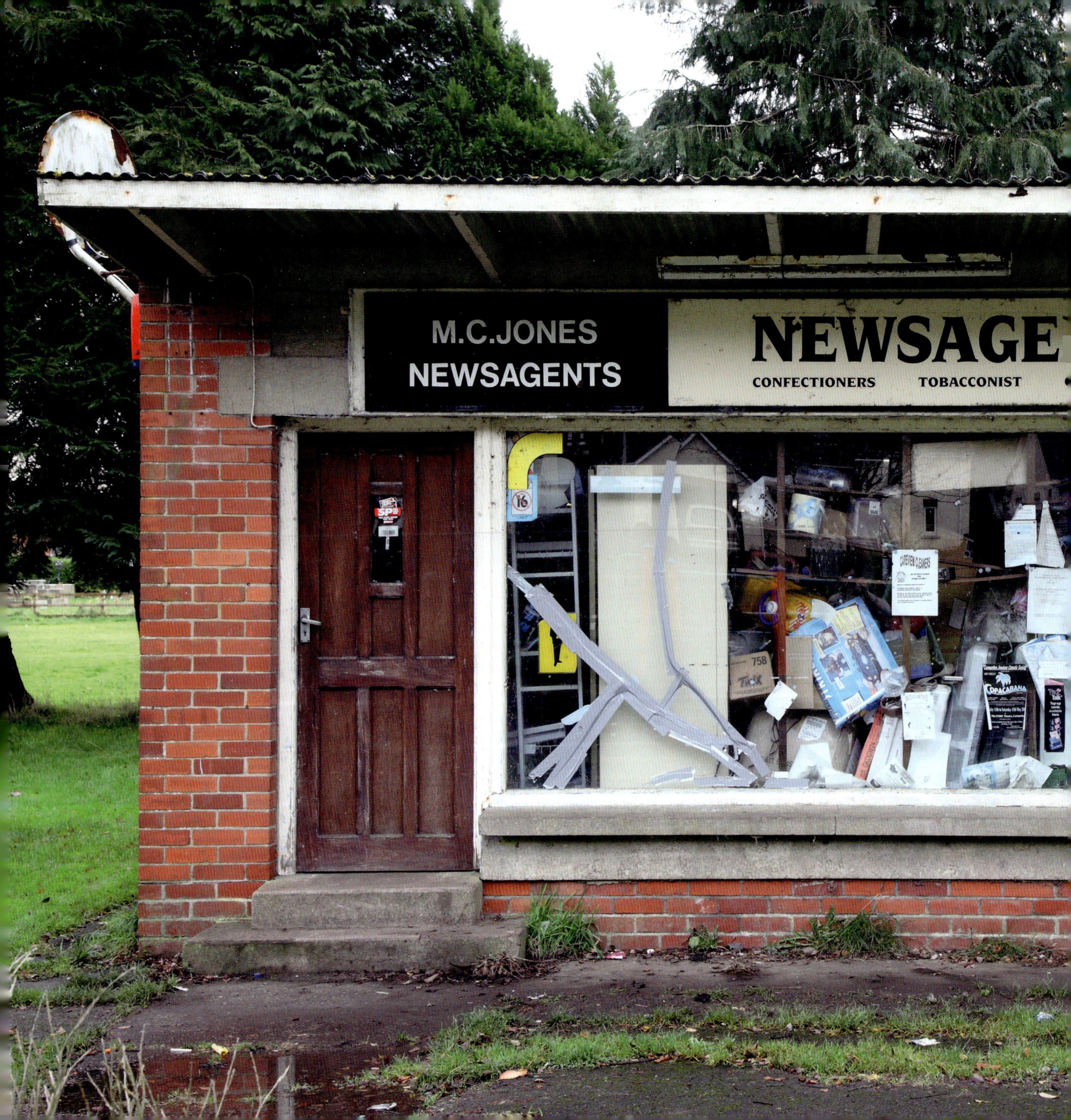

M.C.JONES
NEWSAGENTS
NEWSAGE
CONFECTIONERS   TOBACCONIST

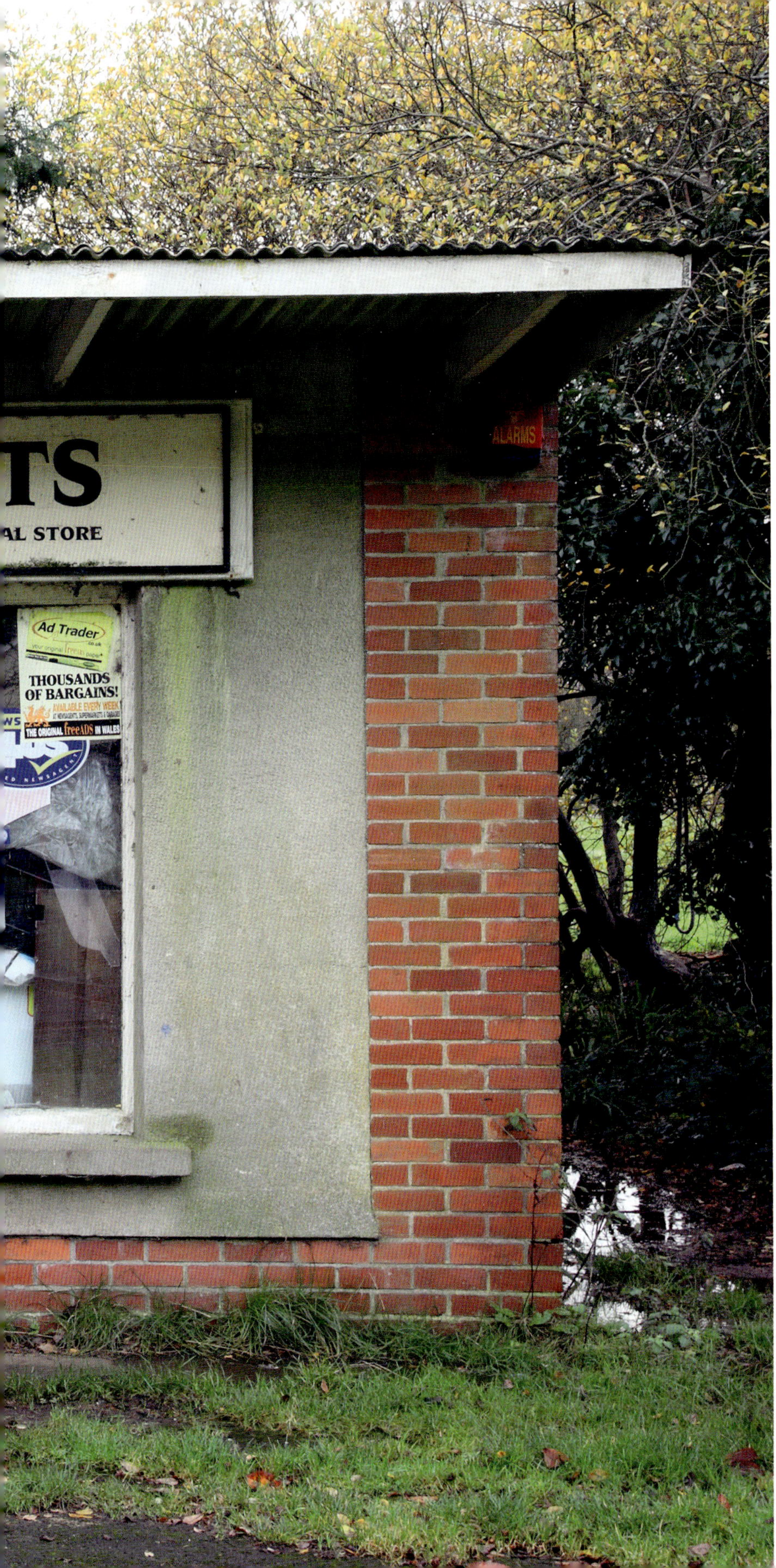

Llanmiloe, Carmarthenshire, 2011.

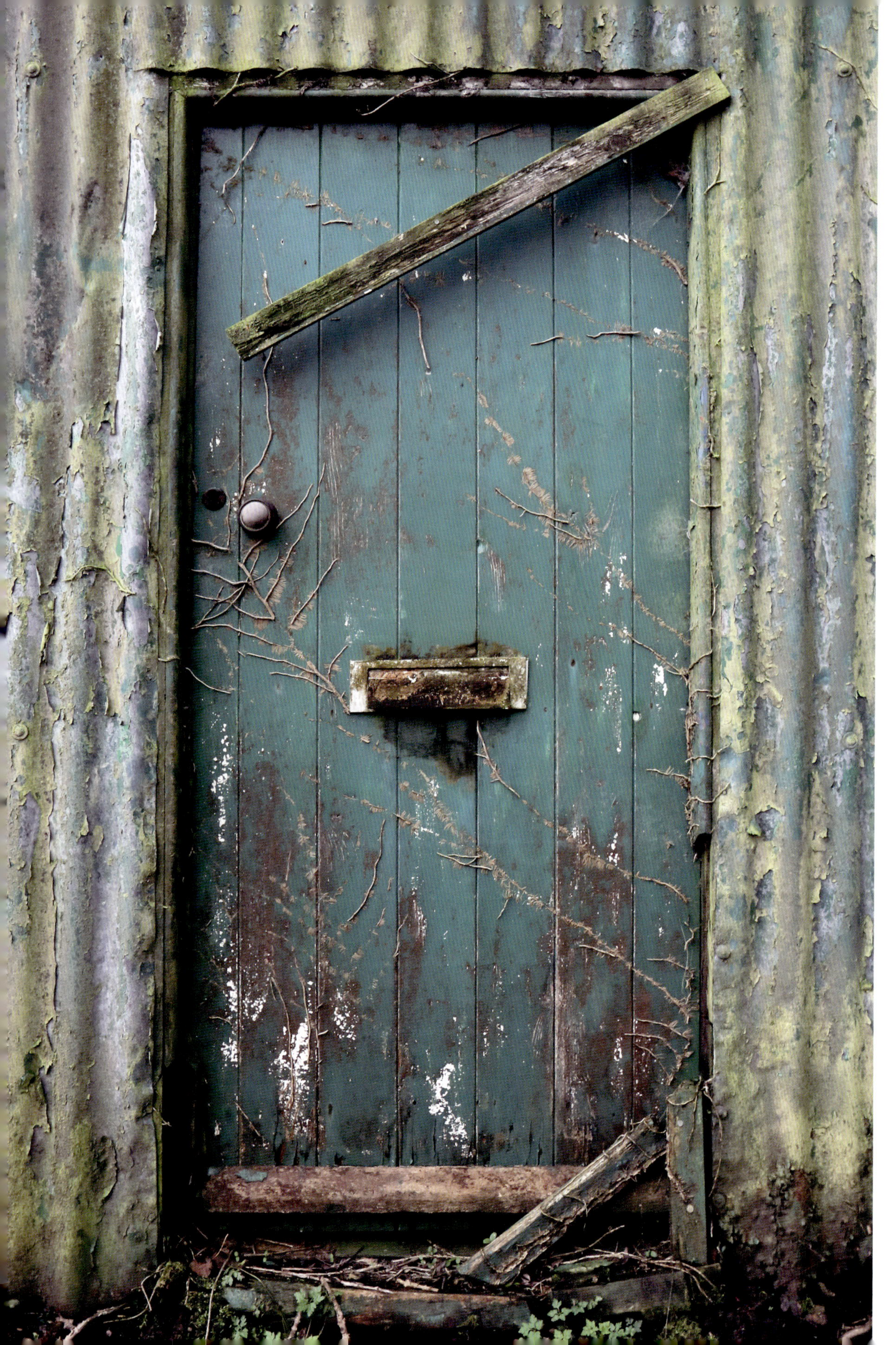

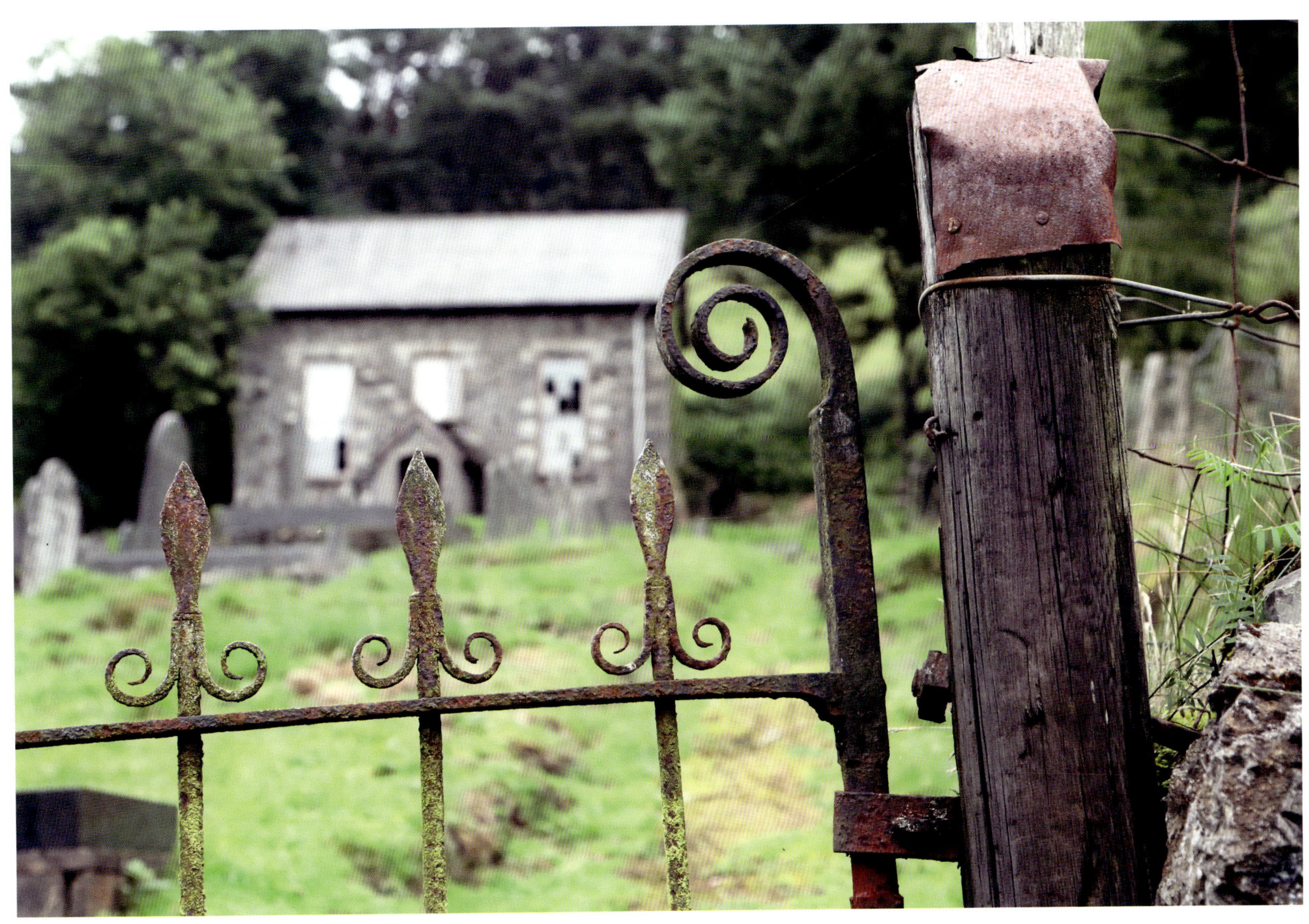

Left: Middle Mill, Pembrokeshire, 2022.

Above: Cwmsymlog, Ceredigion, 2016.

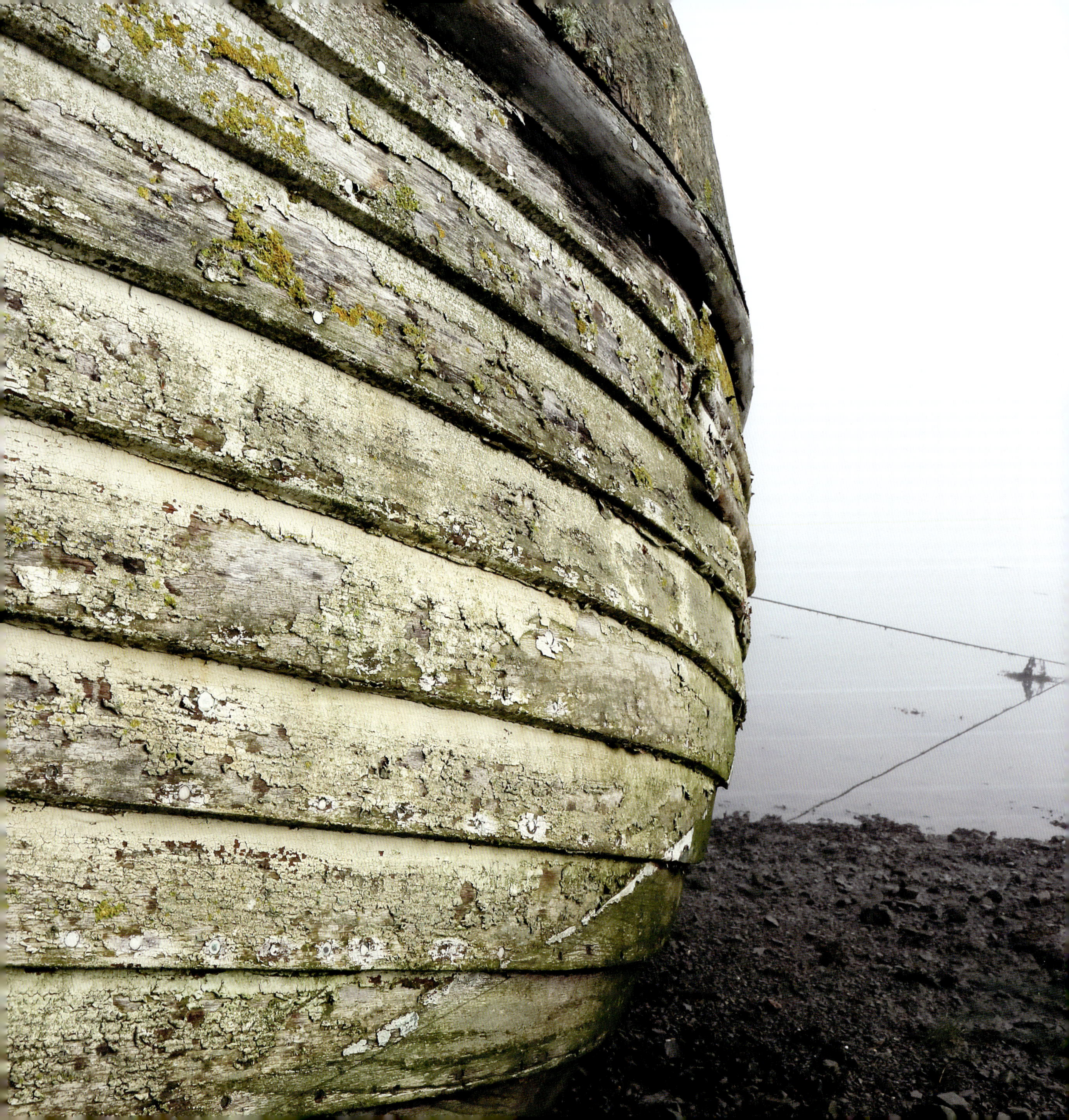

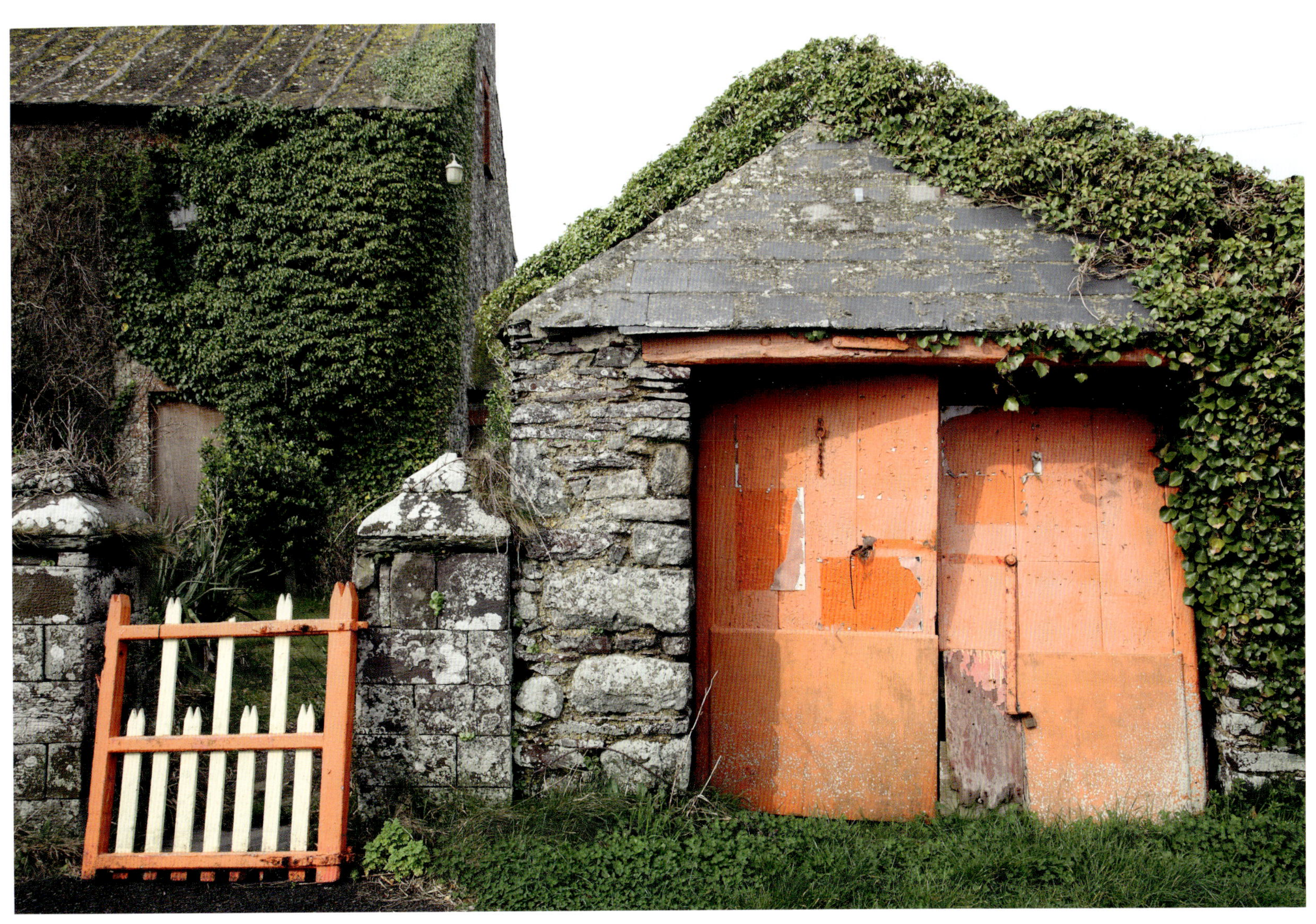

Left: Llangwm, Pembrokeshire, 2018.

Above: Porthclais, Pembrokeshire, 2012.

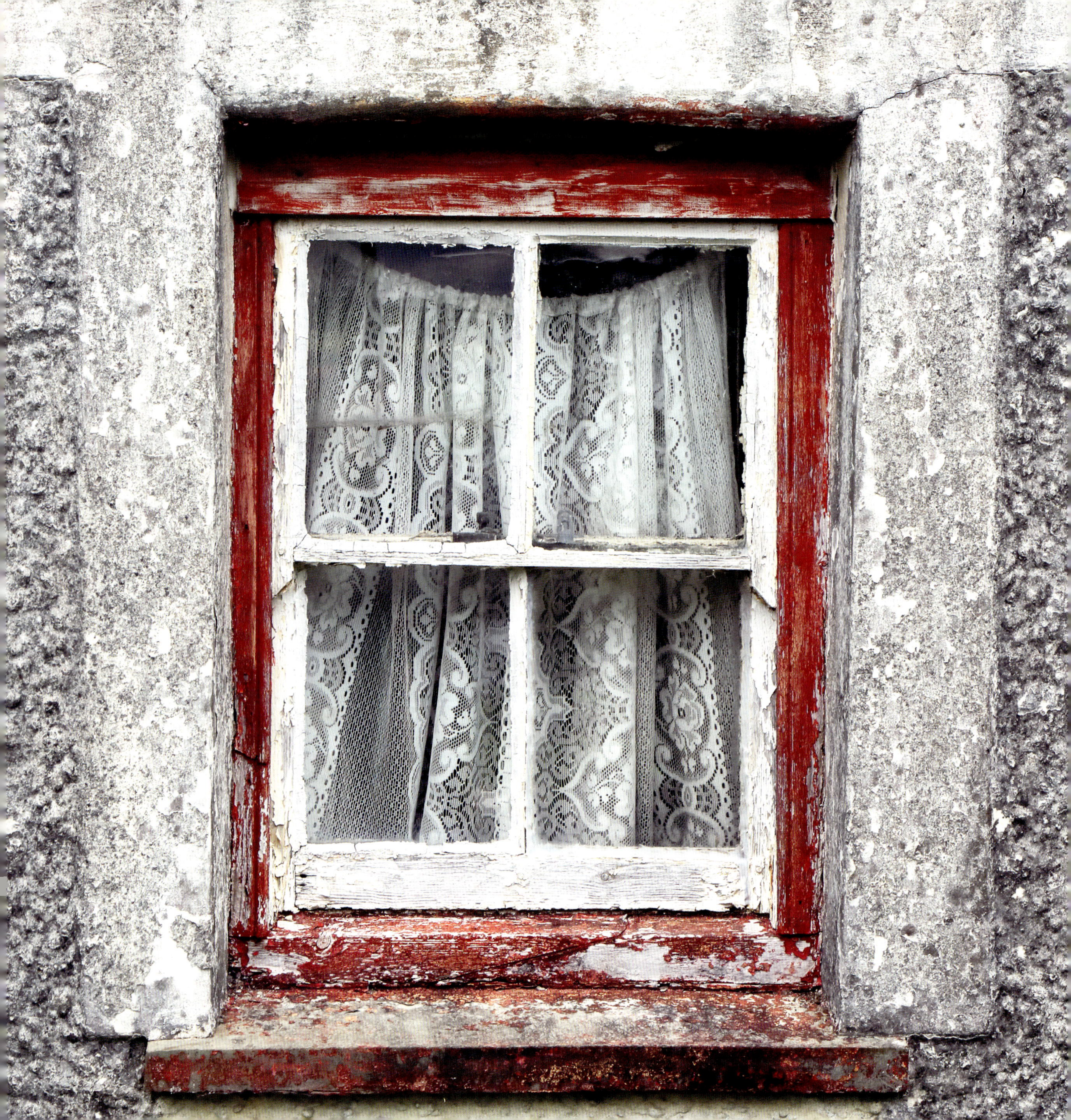

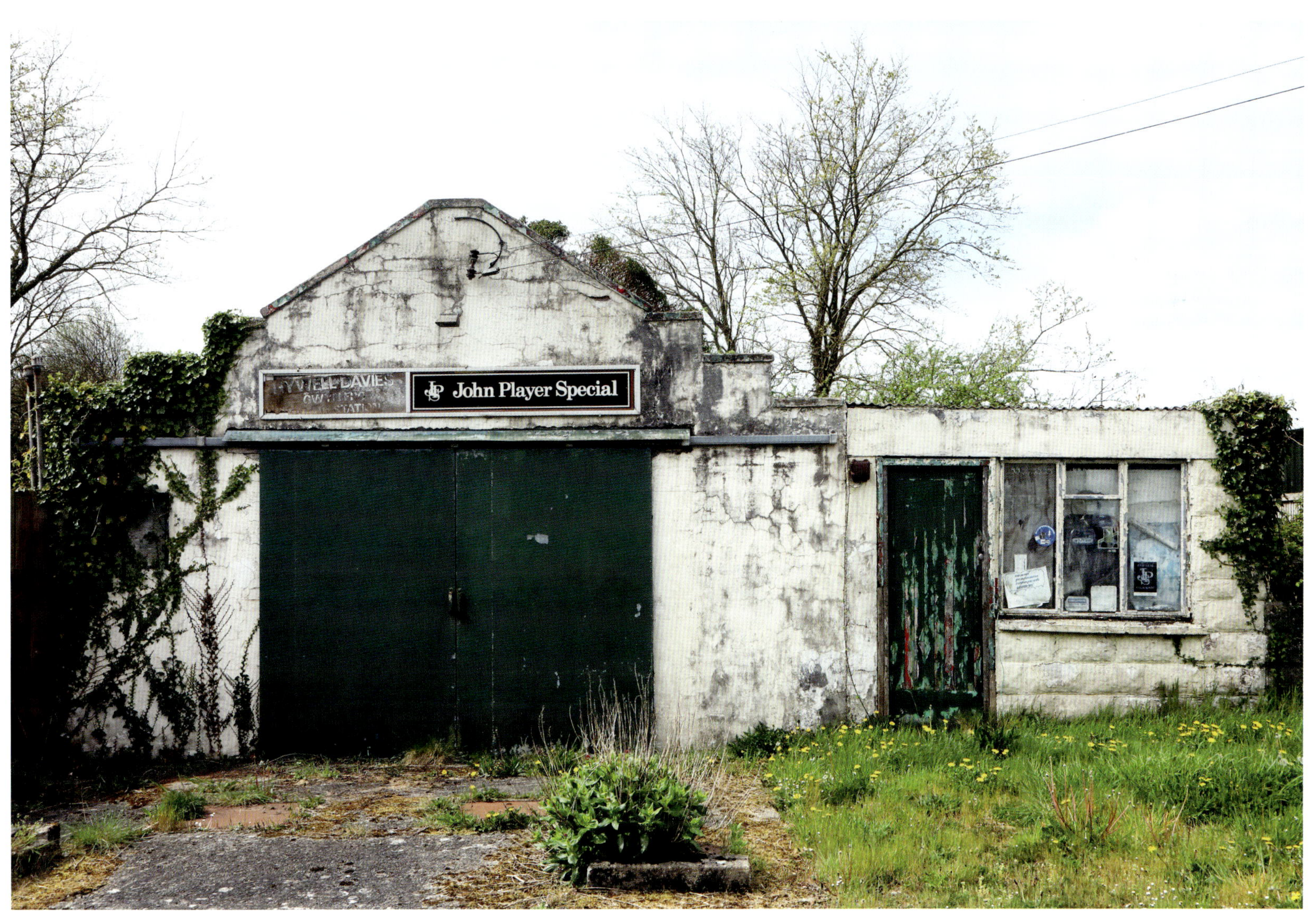

Left: Wolfscastle, Pembrokeshire, 2022.

Above: Ferwig, Ceredigion, 2022.

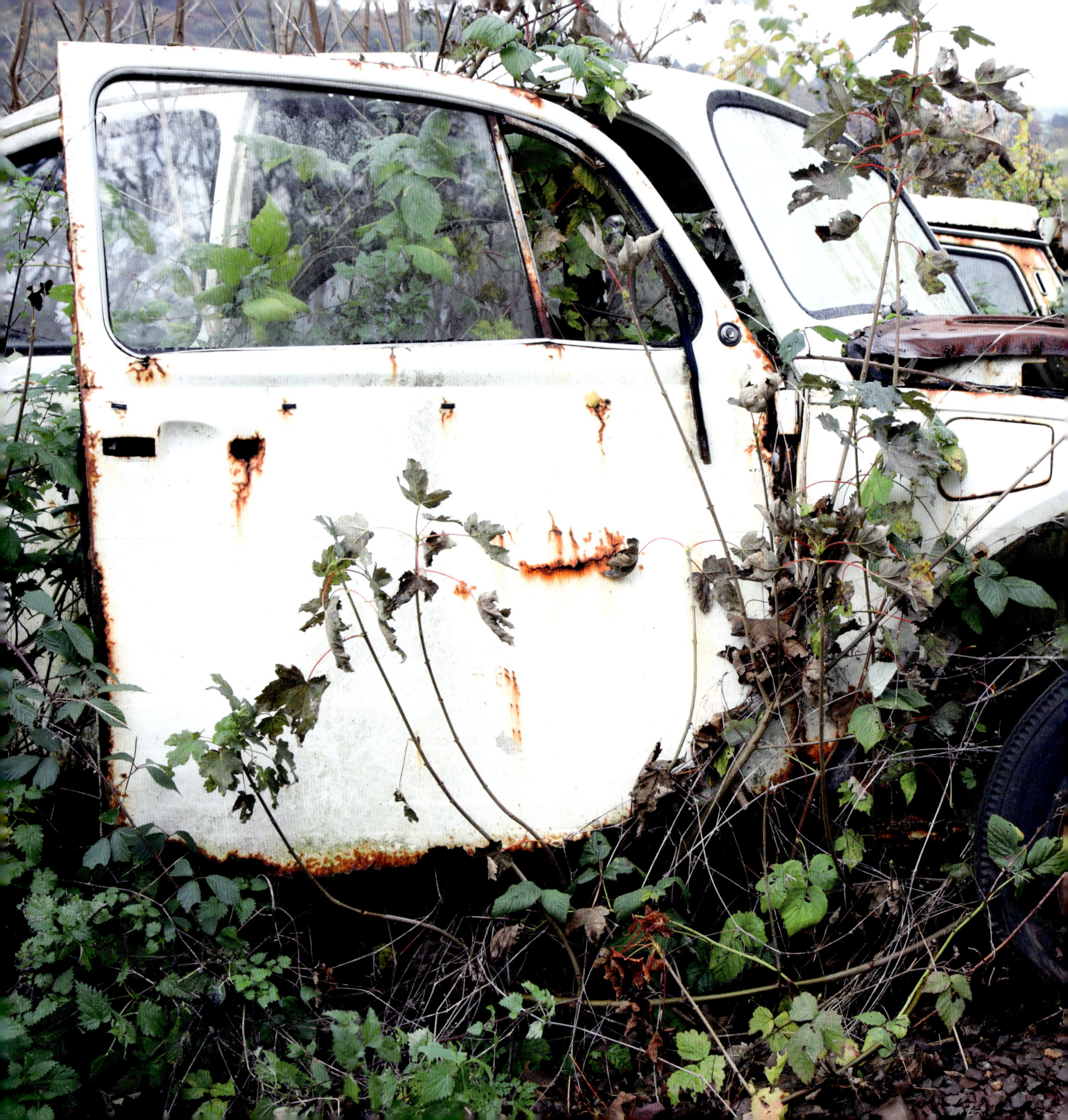

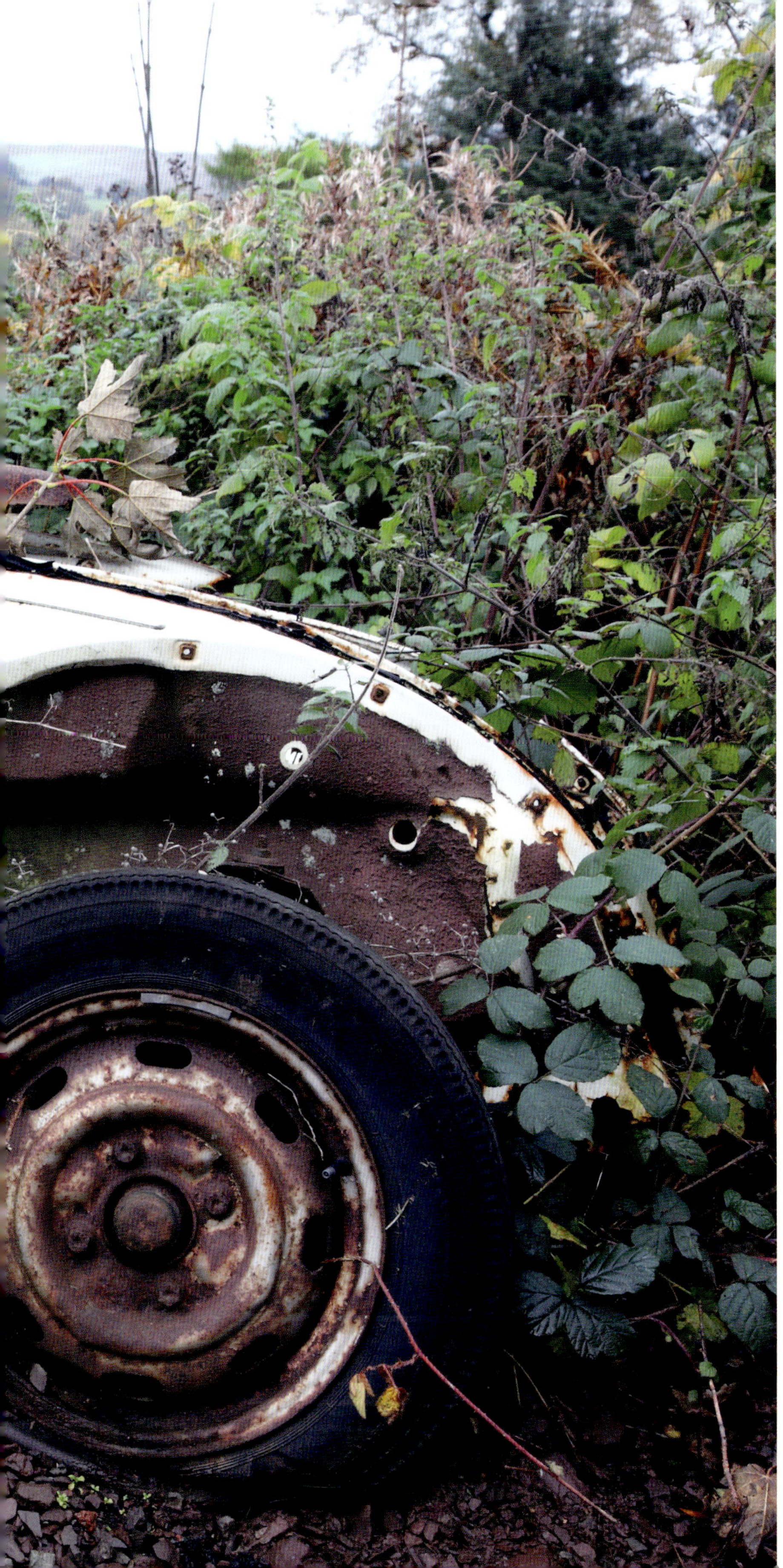

Talybont-on-Usk, Powys, 2010.

Pages 68-69: Mynachlogddu,
Pembrokeshire, 2013.

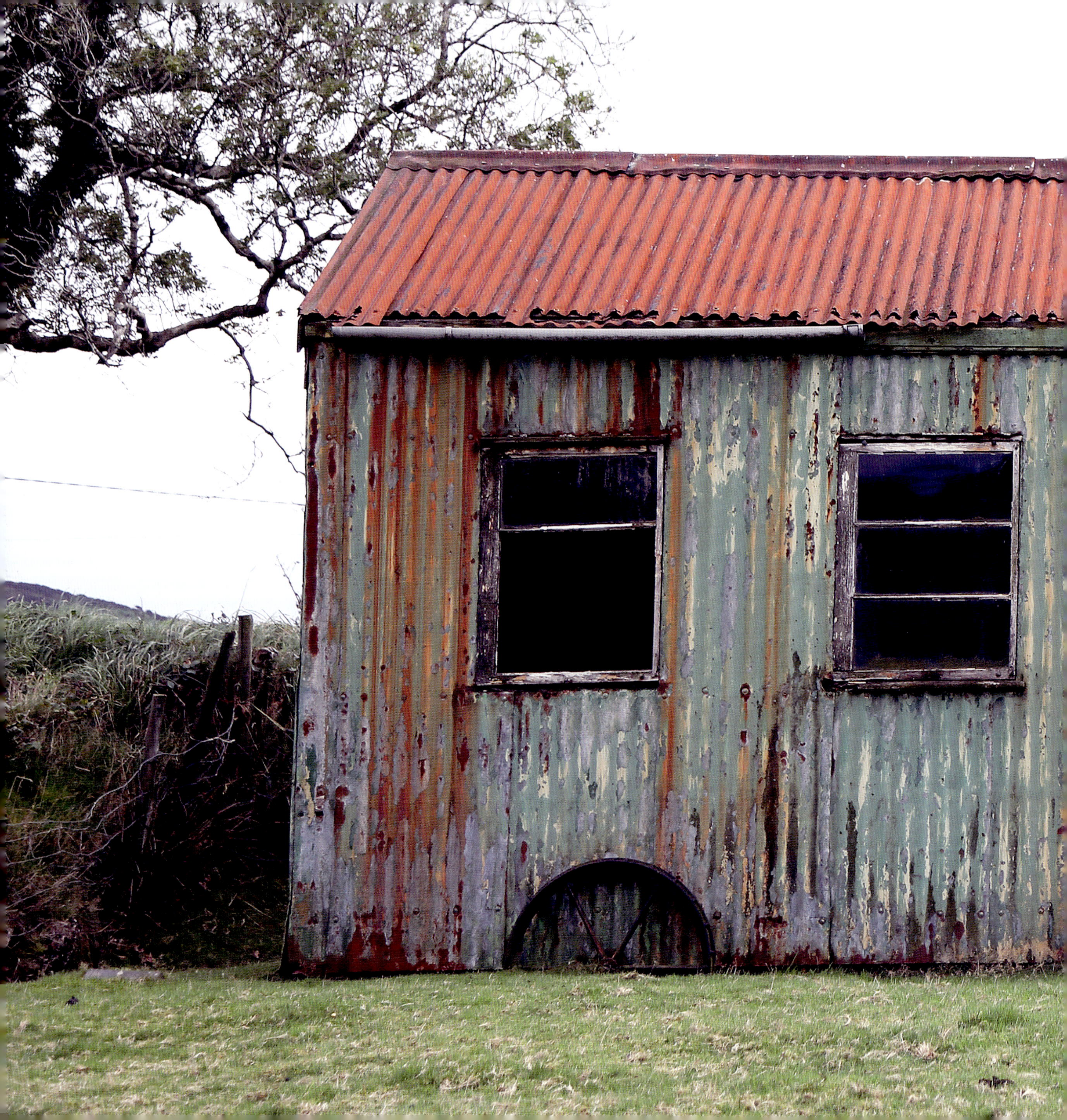

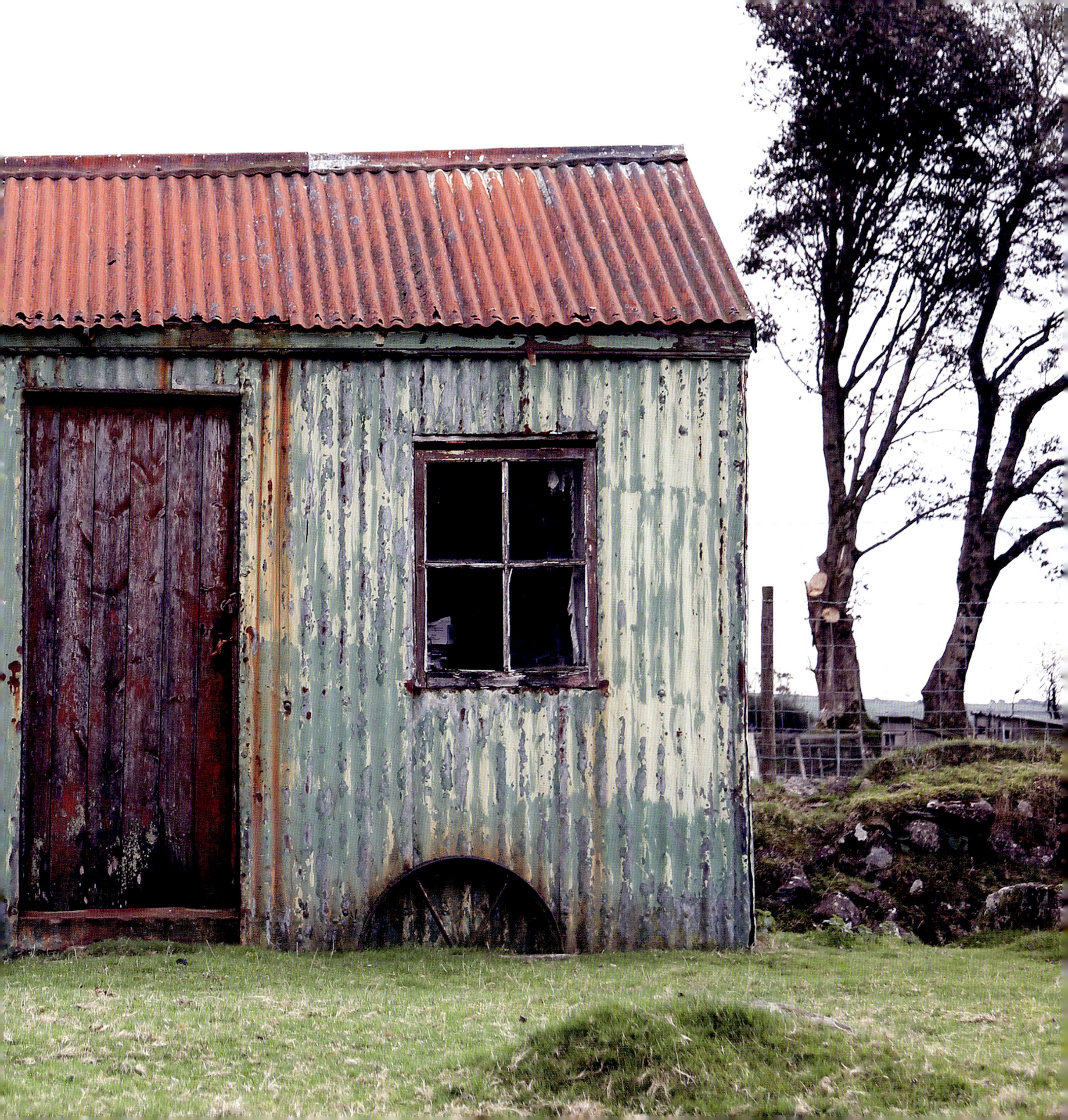

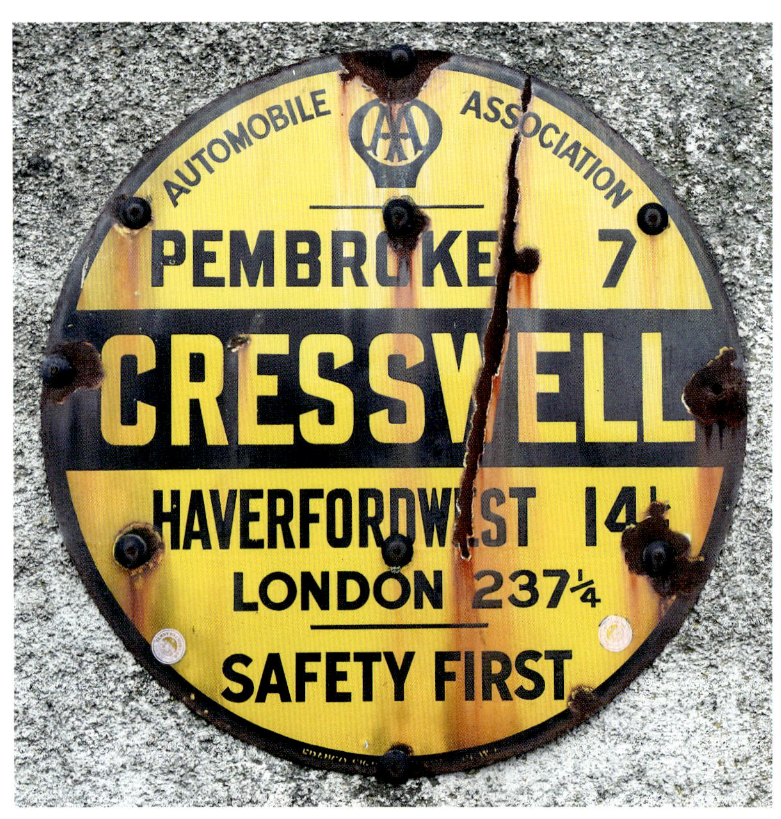
AUTOMOBILE ASSOCIATION
PEMBROKE 7
CRESSWELL
HAVERFORDWEST 14¼
LONDON 237¼
SAFETY FIRST

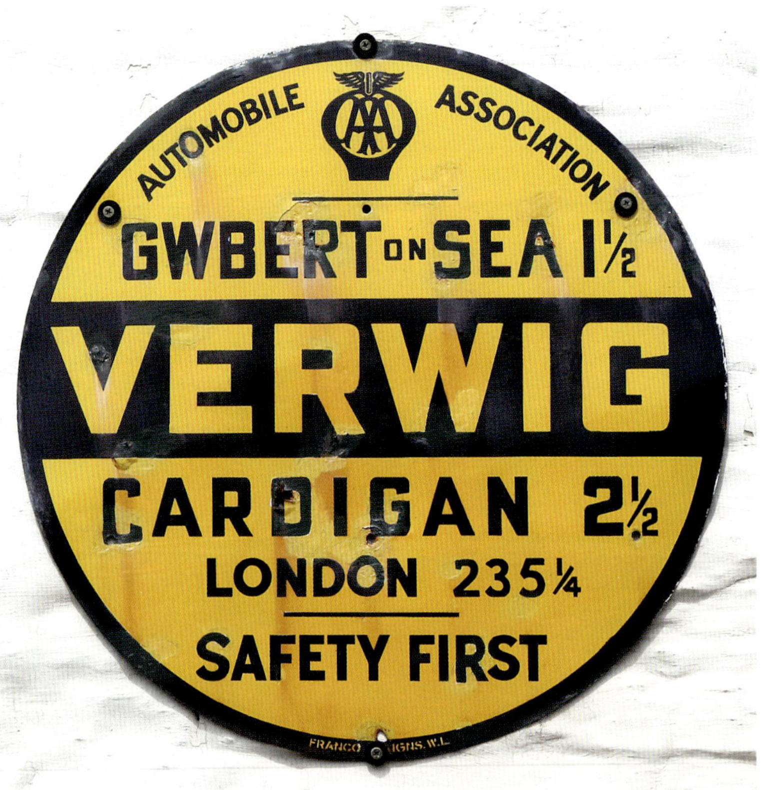
AUTOMOBILE ASSOCIATION
GWBERT ON SEA 1½
VERWIG
CARDIGAN 2½
LONDON 235¼
SAFETY FIRST

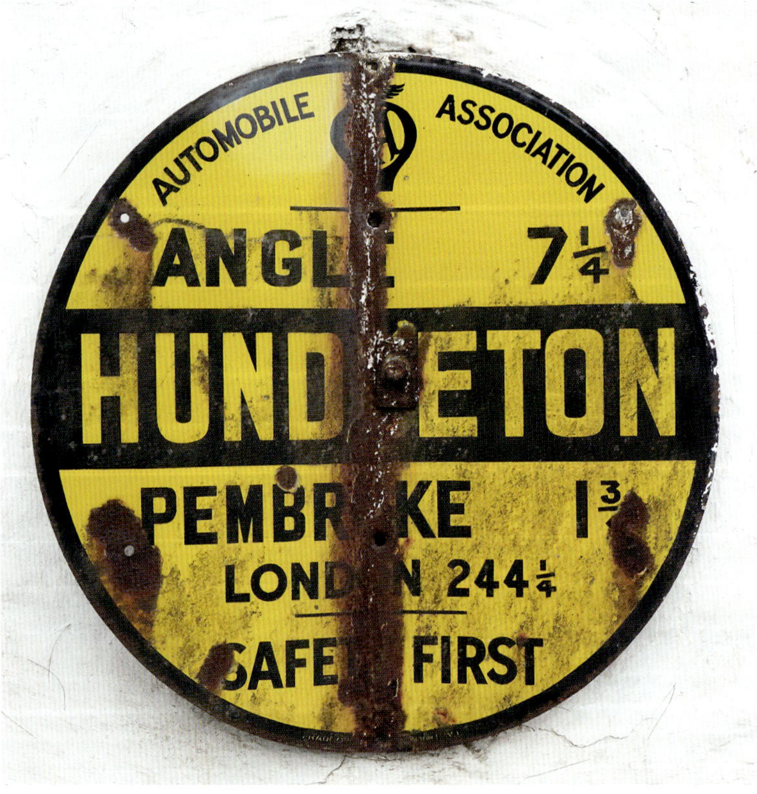
AUTOMOBILE ASSOCIATION
ANGLE 7¼
HUNDLETON
PEMBROKE 1¾
LONDON 244¼
SAFETY FIRST

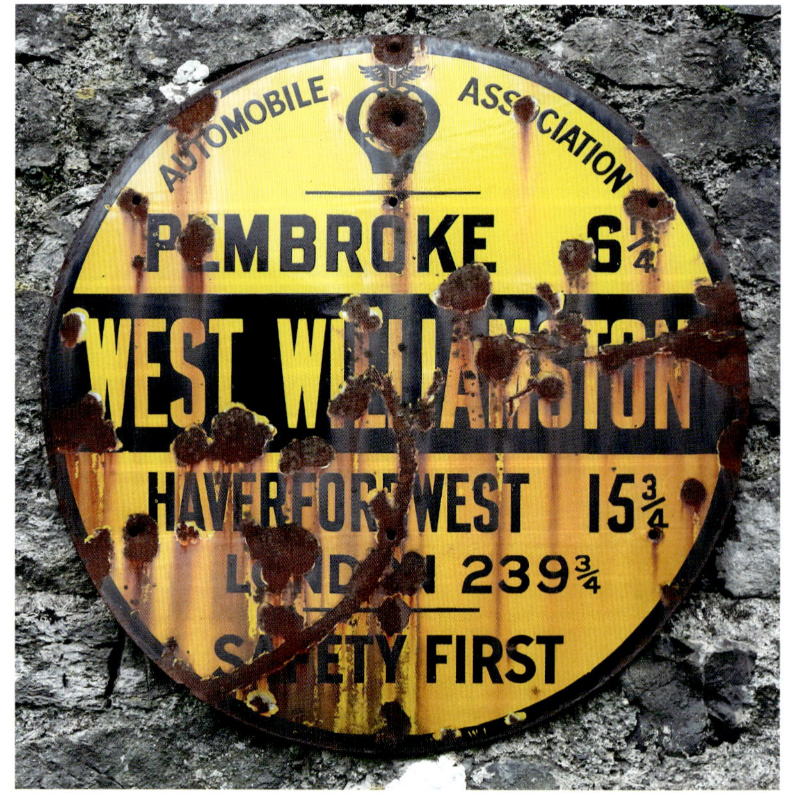
AUTOMOBILE ASSOCIATION
PEMBROKE 6¼
WEST WILLIAMSTON
HAVERFORDWEST 15¾
LONDON 239¾
SAFETY FIRST

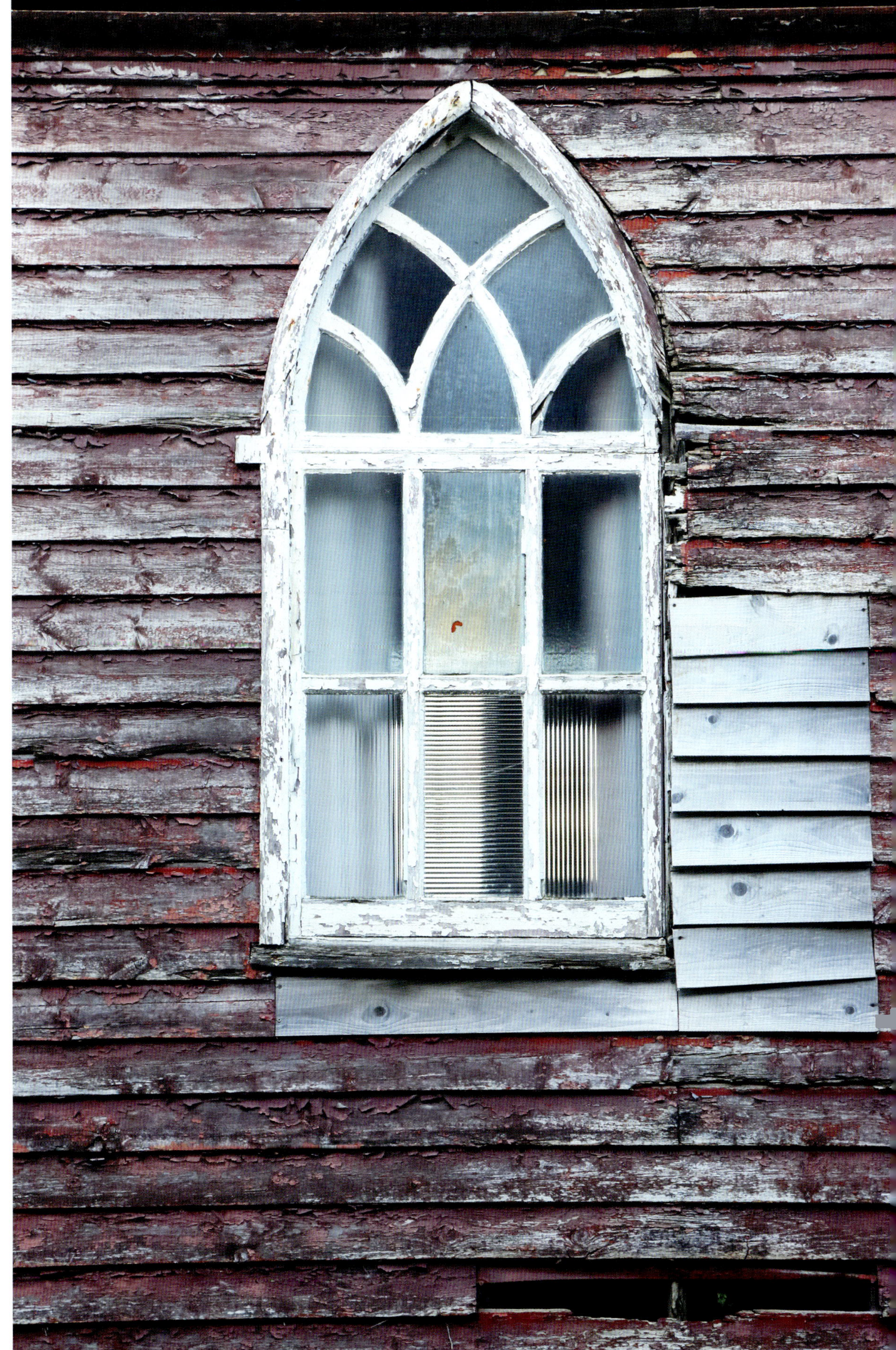

Neyland, Pembrokeshire, 2023.

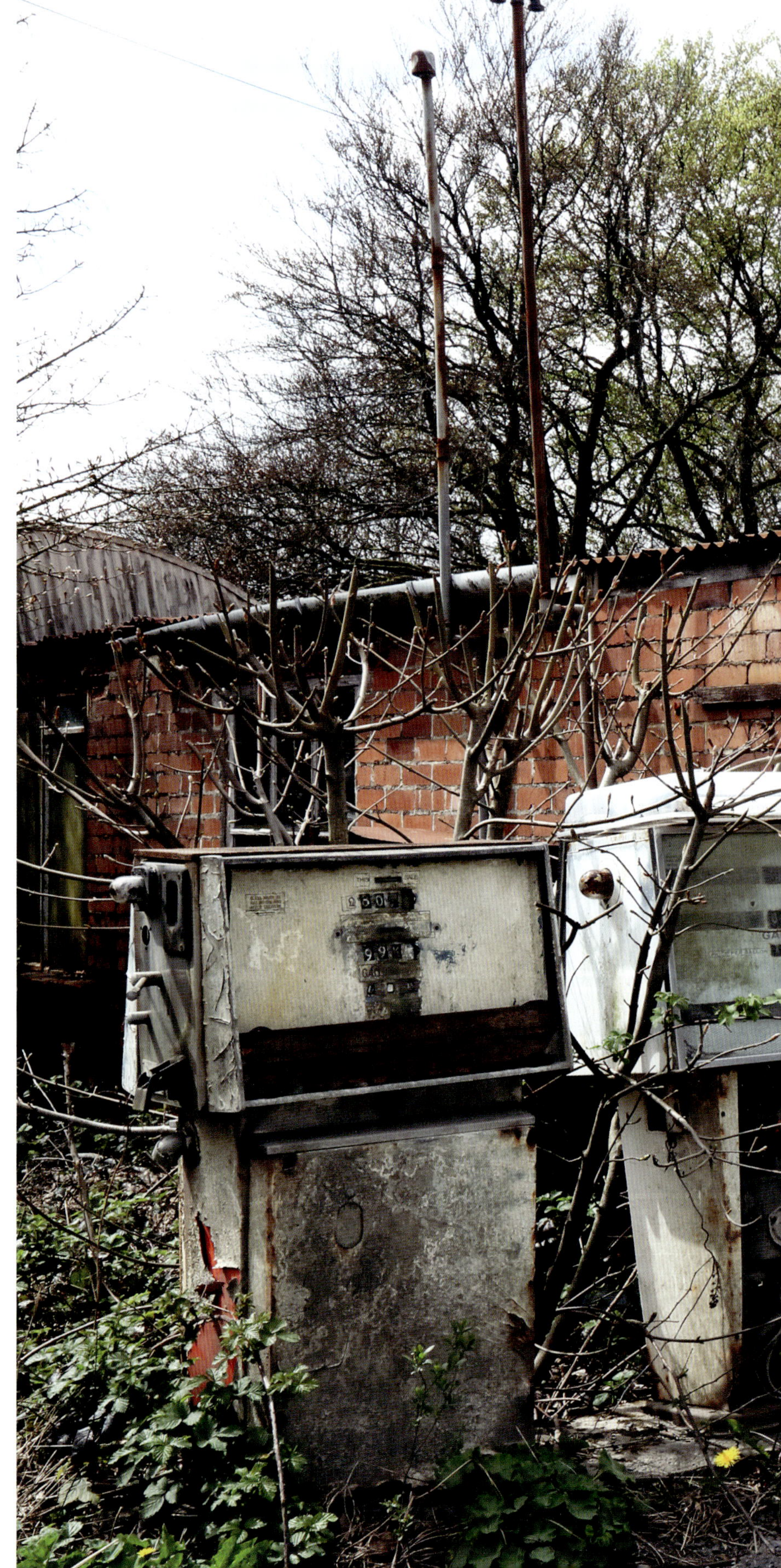

Gorsgoch, Ceredigion, 2022.

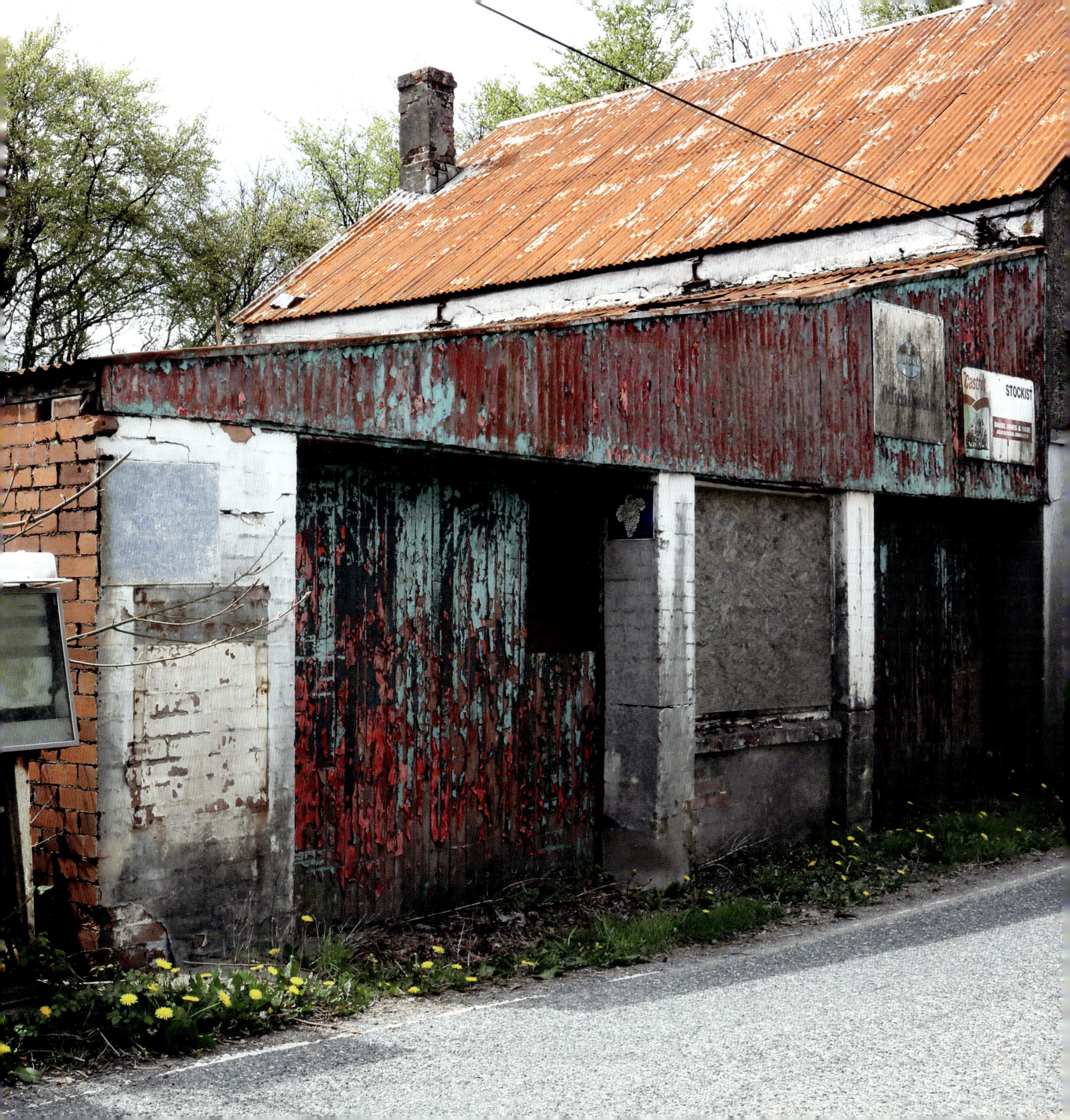
Castrol
STOCKIST
DANIEL JONES & SONS

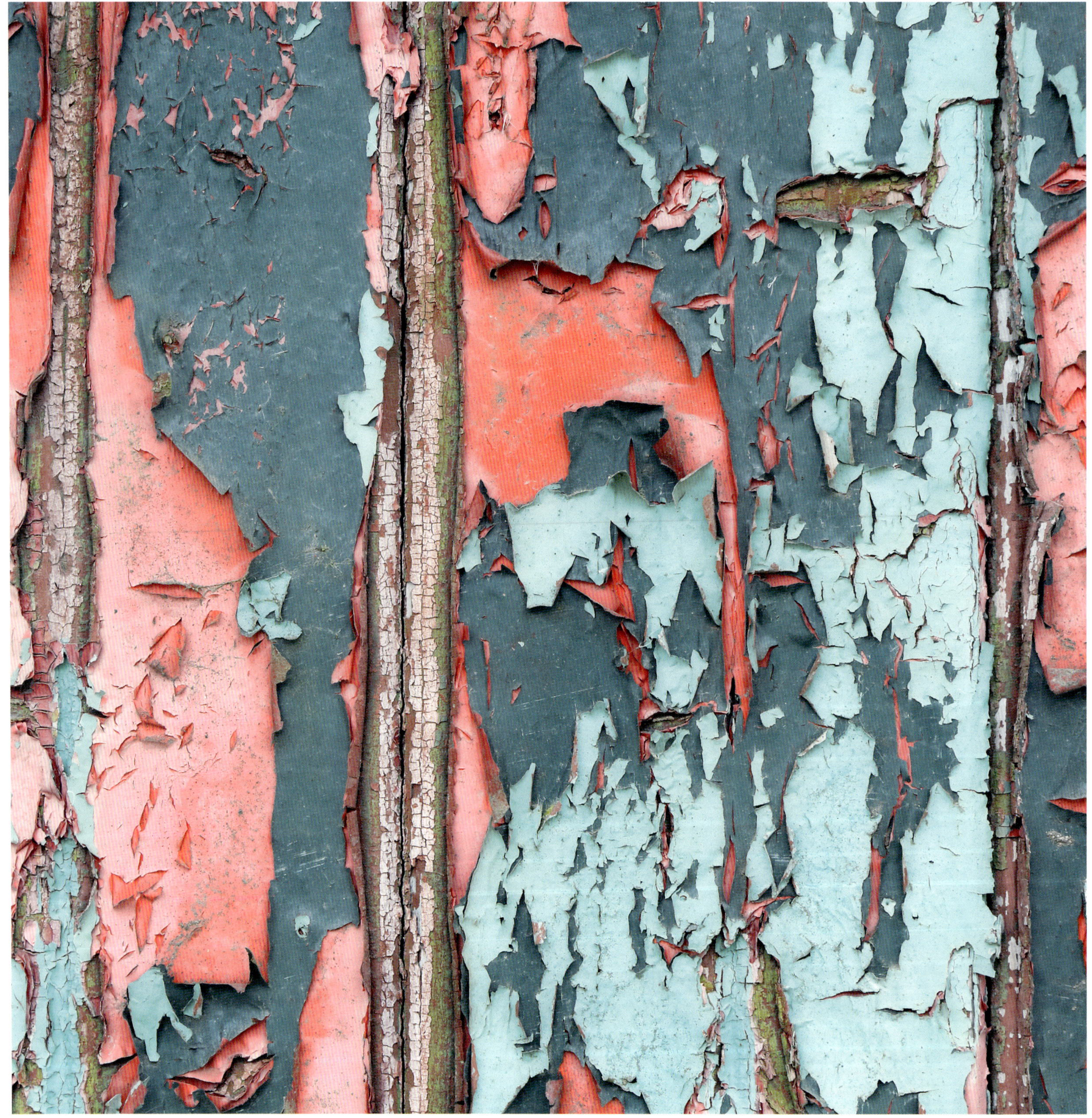

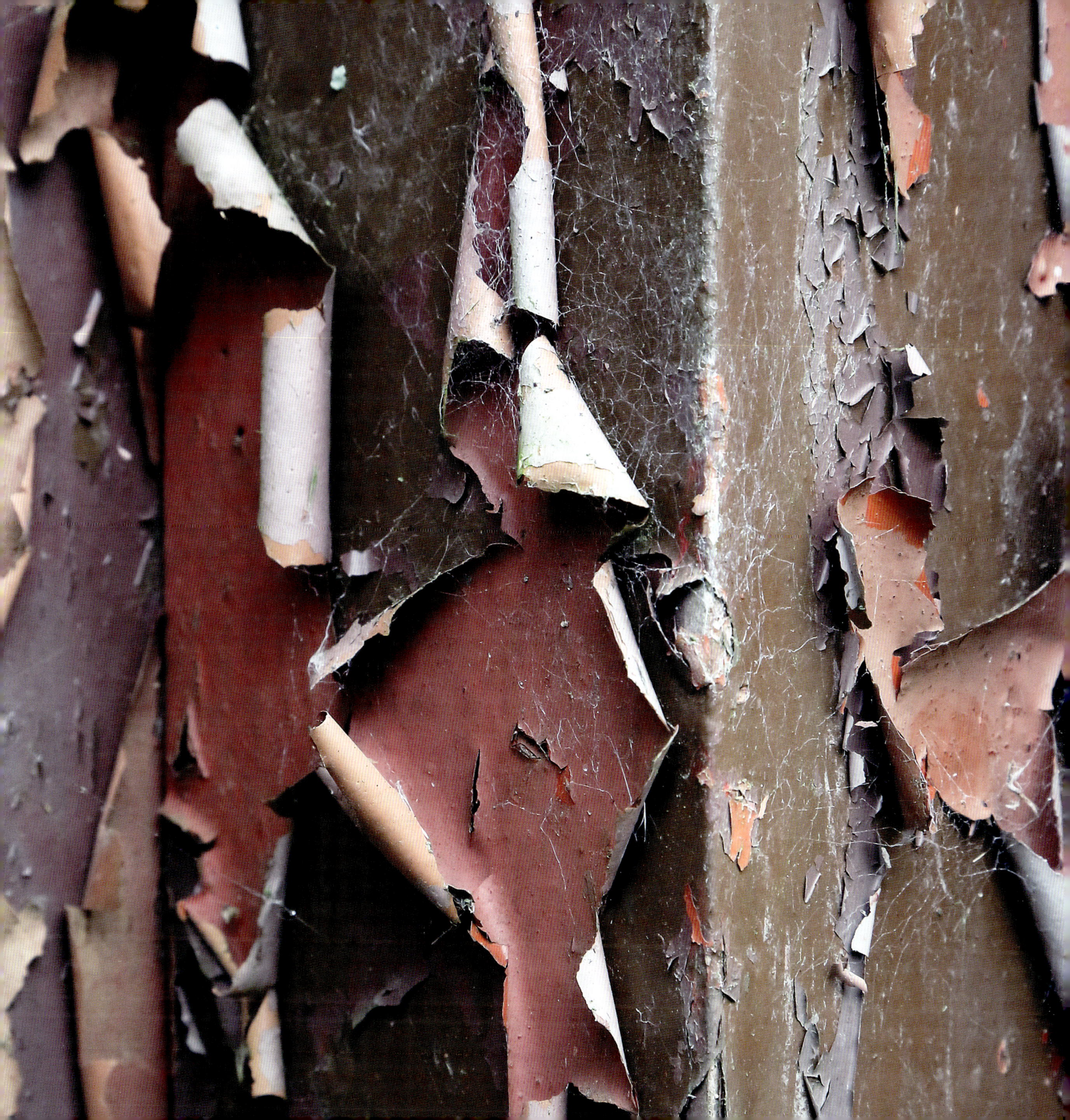

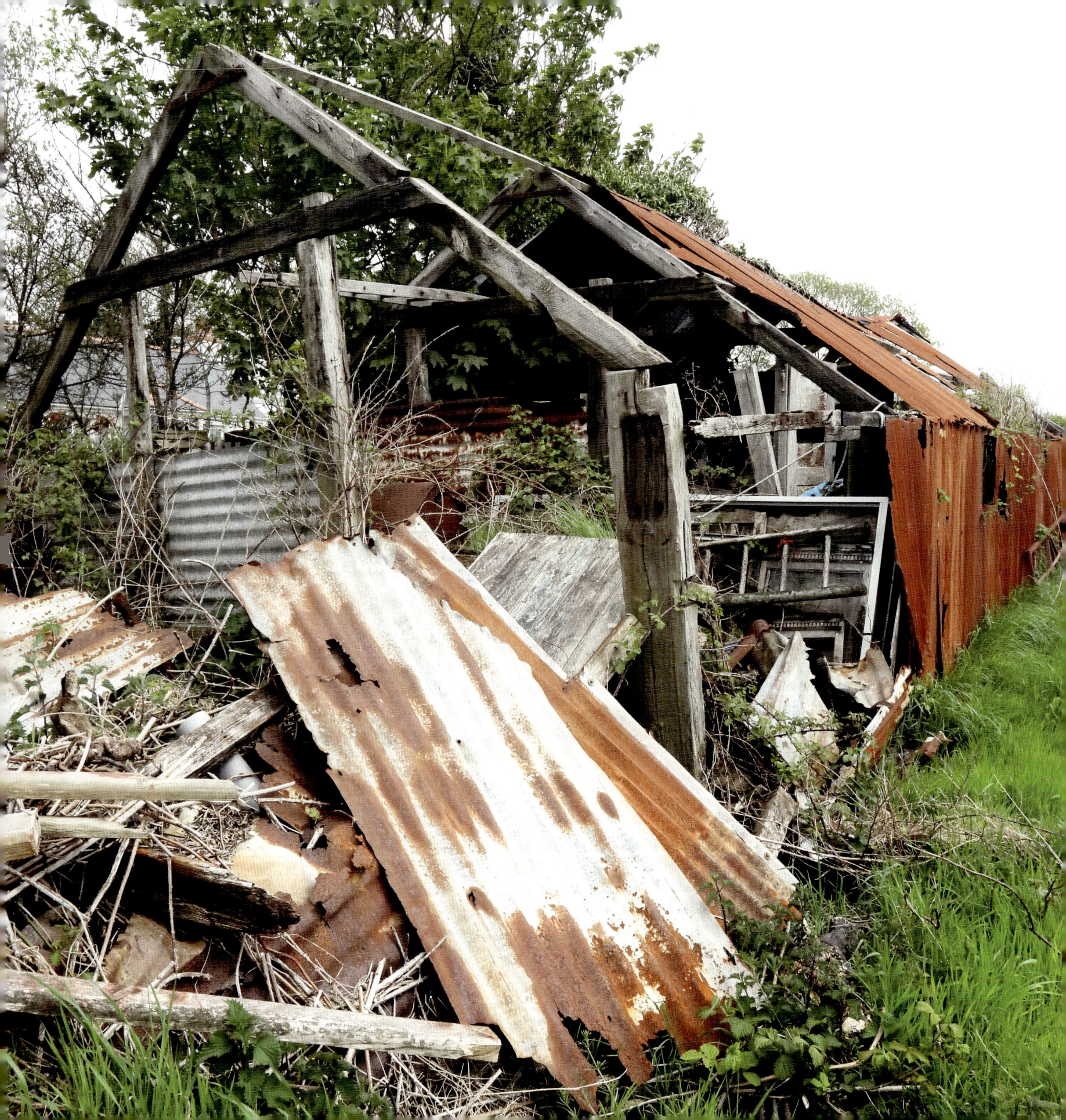

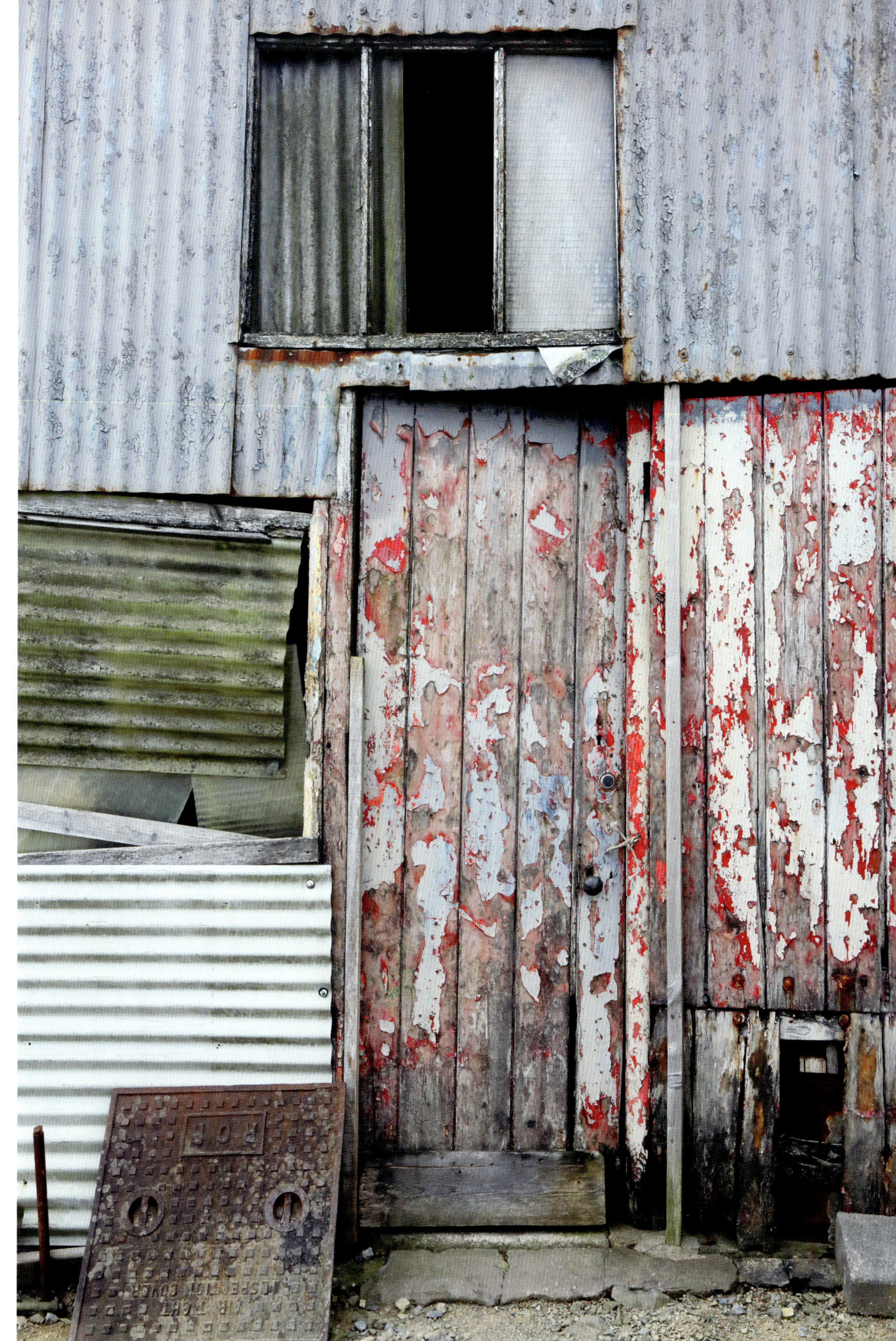

Left: Llangwm,
Pembrokeshire, 2023.

Right: Trelech,
Carmarthenshire, 2022.

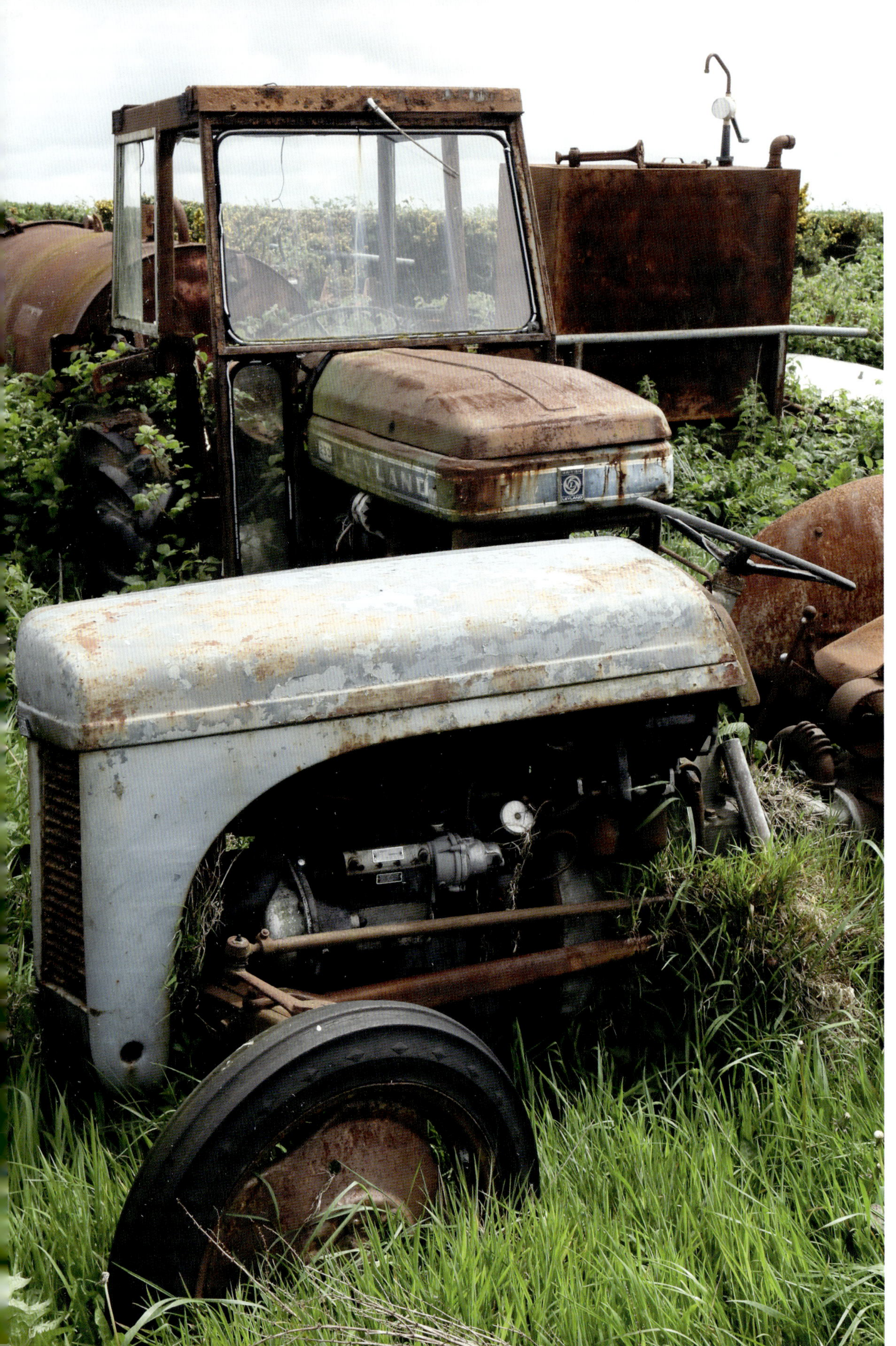

Left: Pembrokeshire, 2022.

Right: Llanrug, Gwynedd, 2012.

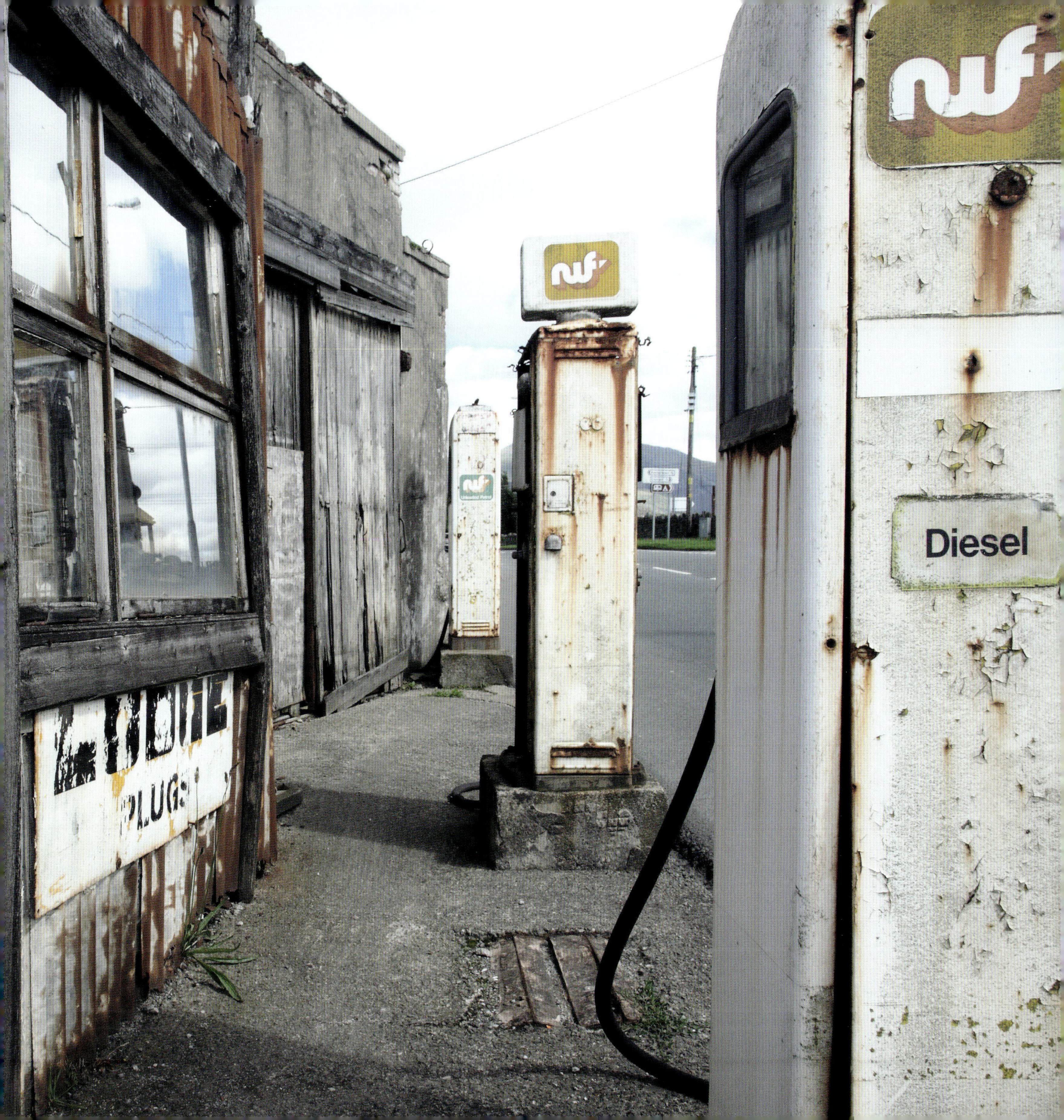
nif
nif
Unleaded Petrol
nif
Diesel
PLUGS

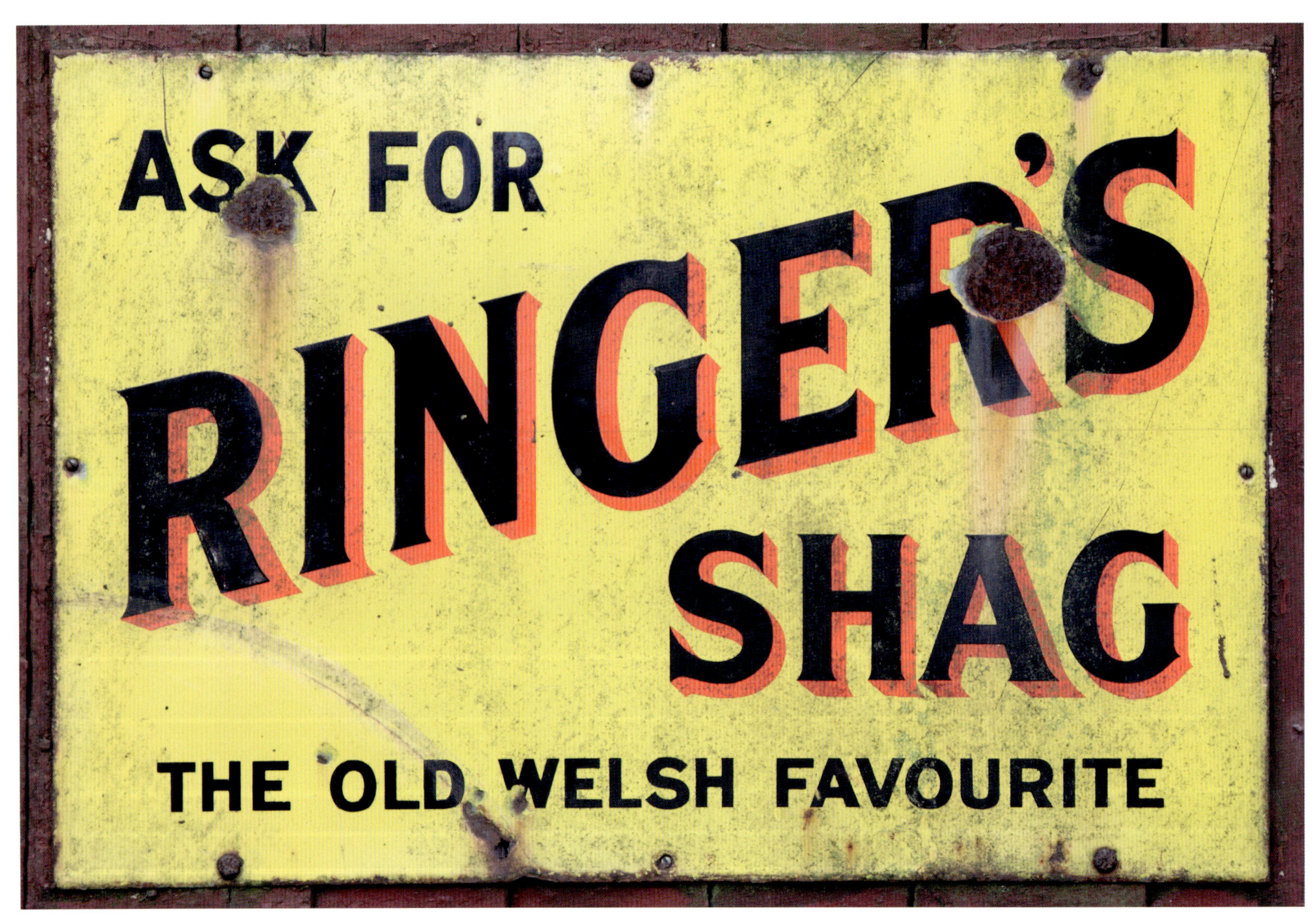

Tufton, Pembrokeshire, 2008.

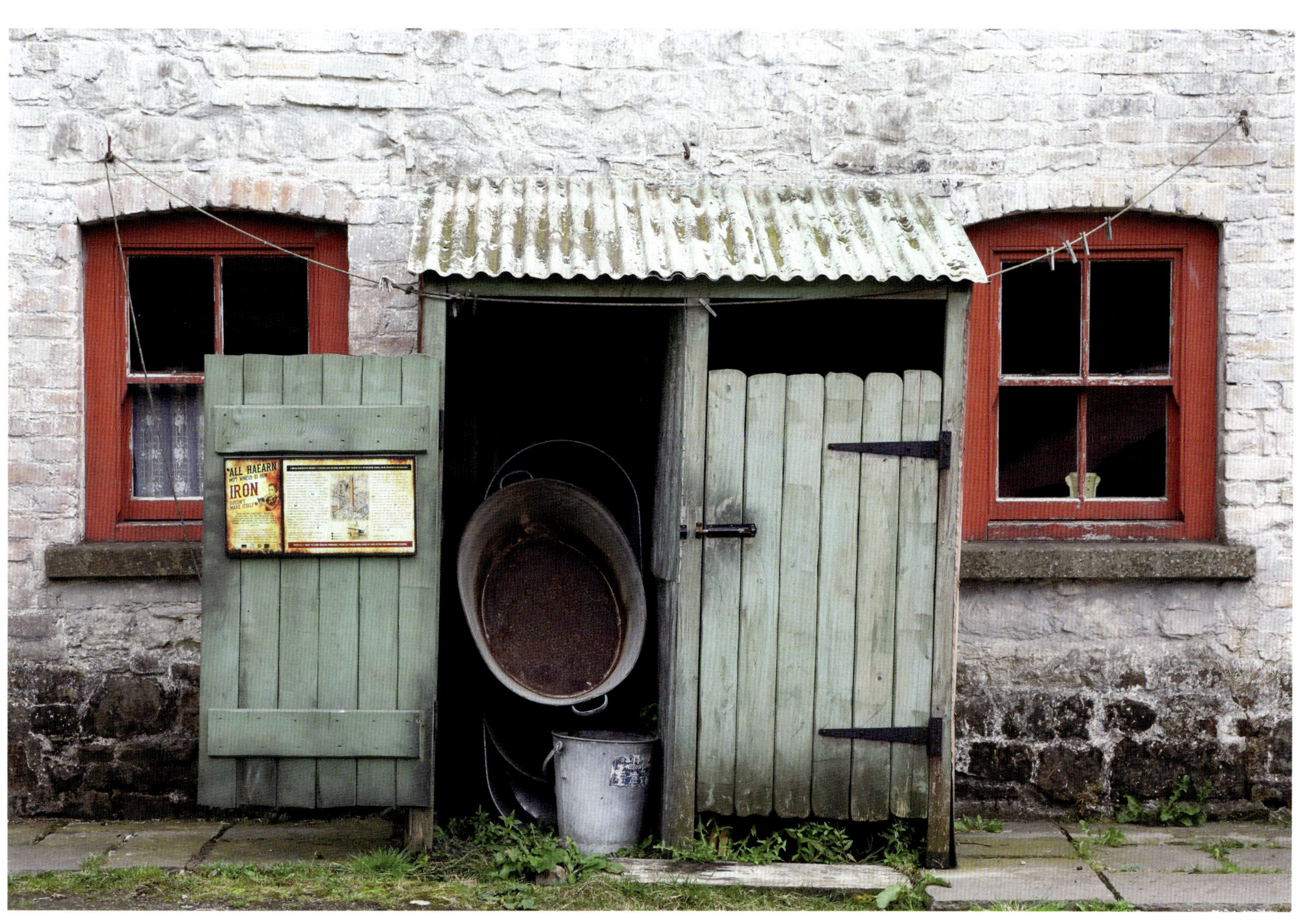

Blaenavon Ironworks, Gwent, 2014.

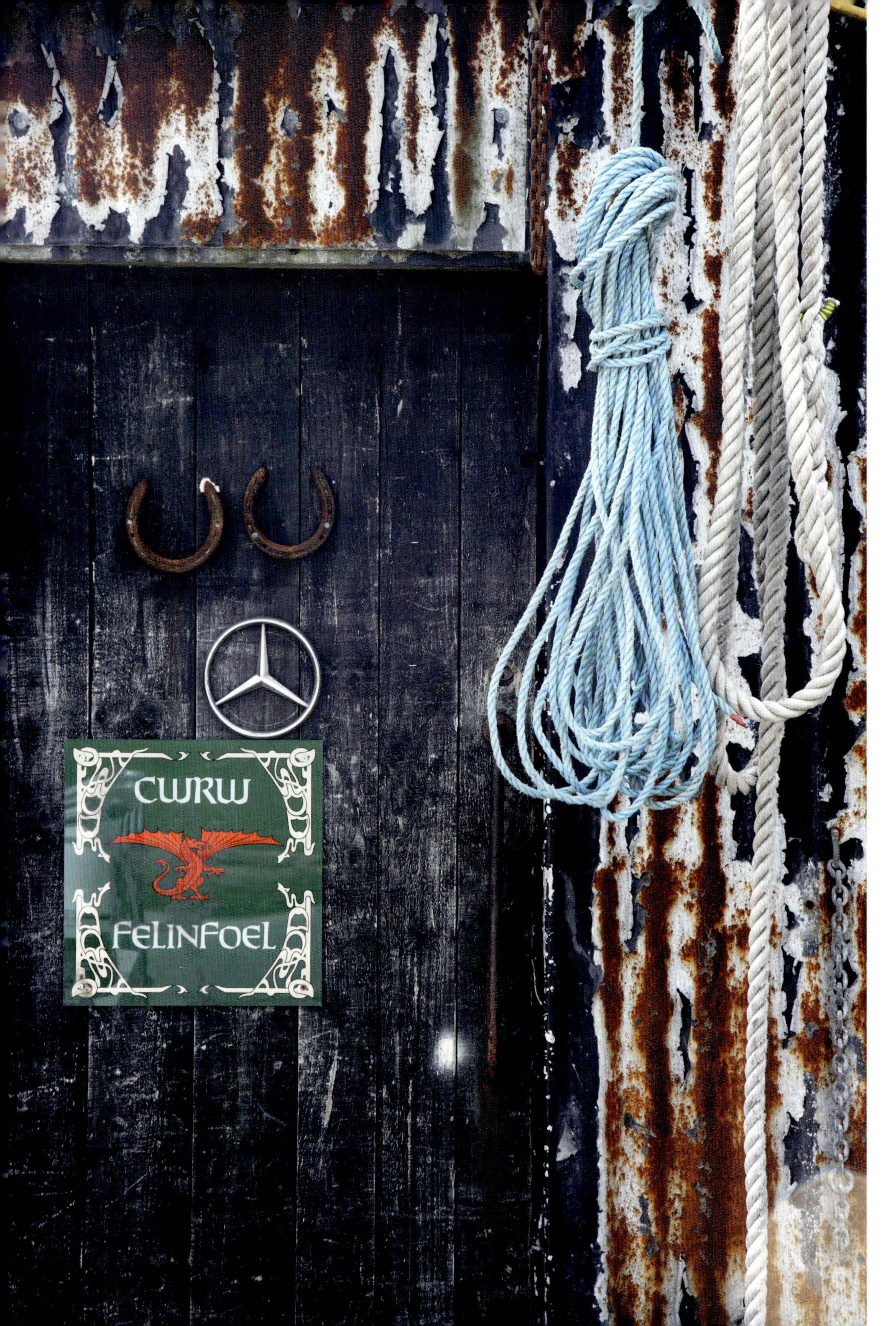

CWRW
FELINFOEL

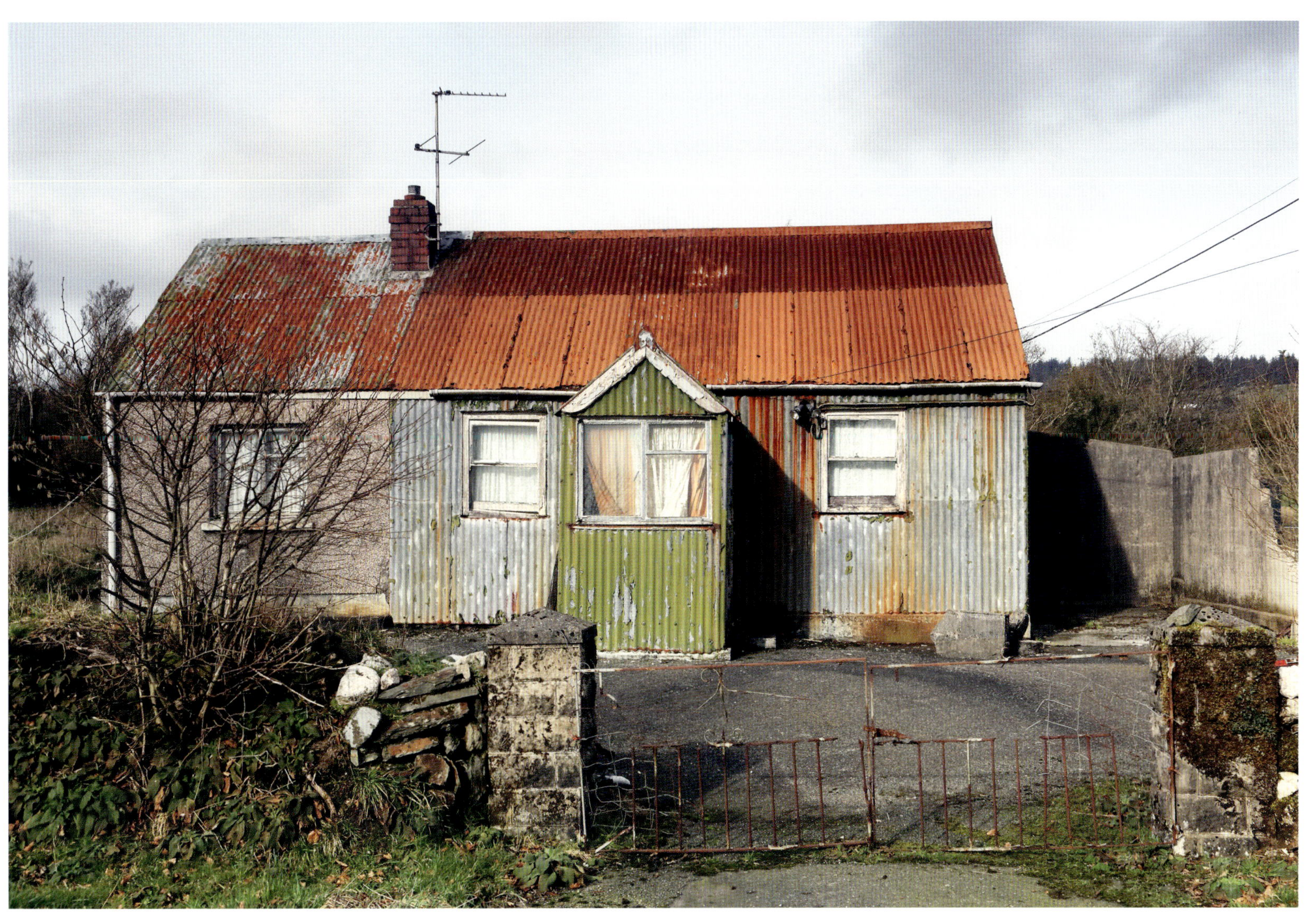

Left: Porthgain, Pembrokeshire, 2009.

Above: Preseli Hills, Pembrokeshire, 2023.

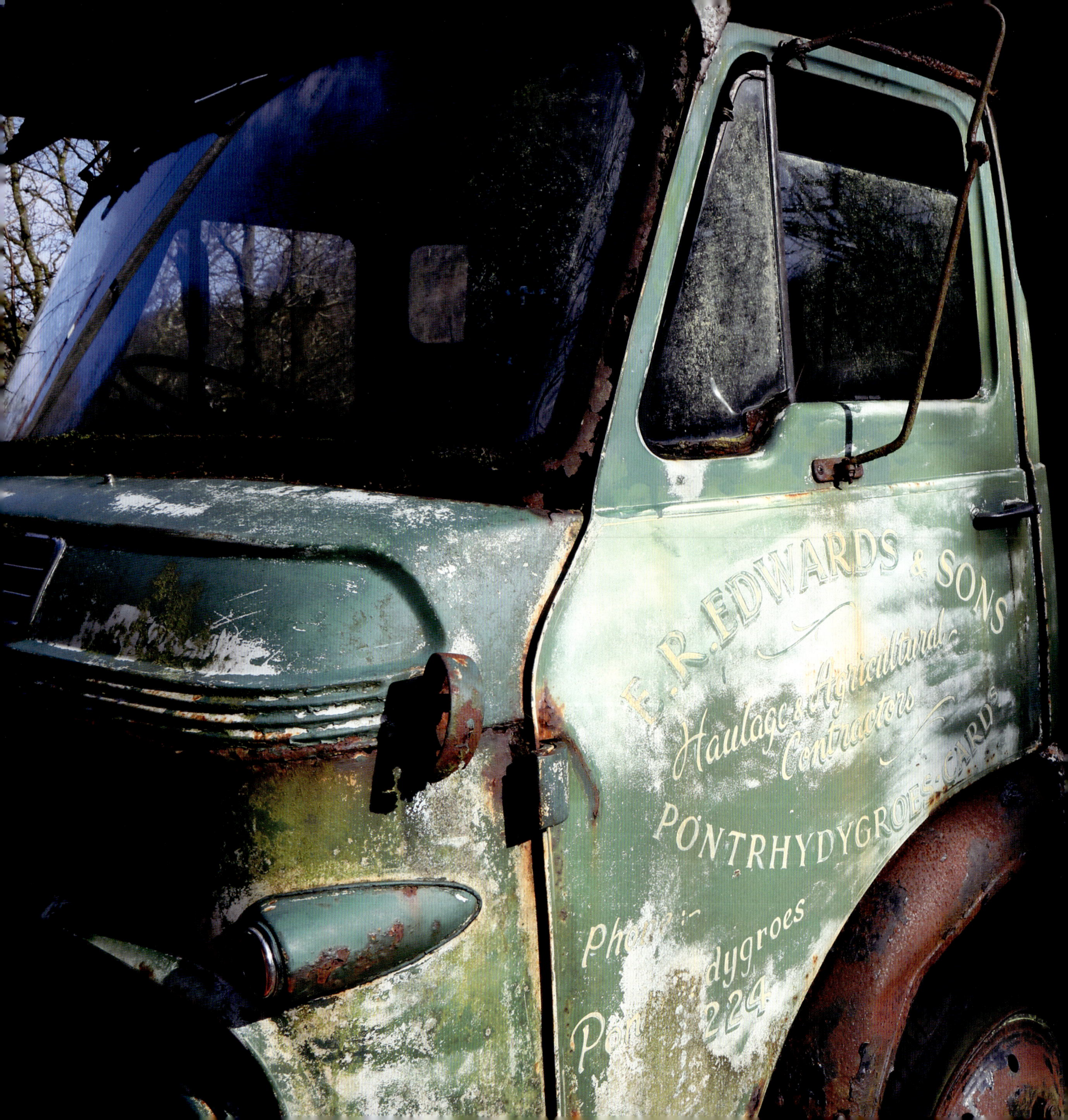
F.R. EDWARDS & SONS
Haulage & Agricultural
Contractors
PONTRHYDYGROES. CARDS.
Phone :-
Pon   dygroes
Pon   224

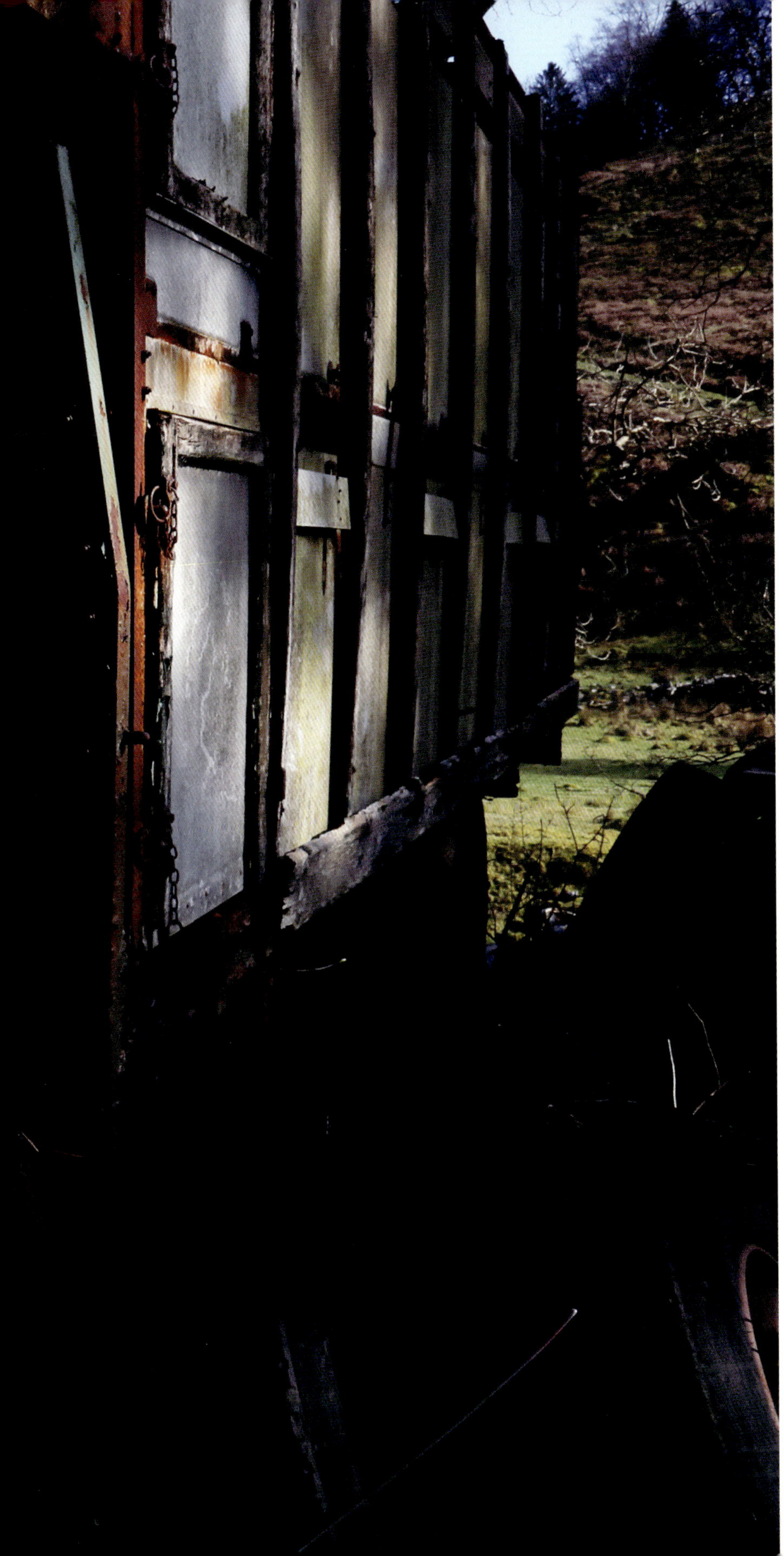

Pontrhydygroes, Ceredigion, 2016.

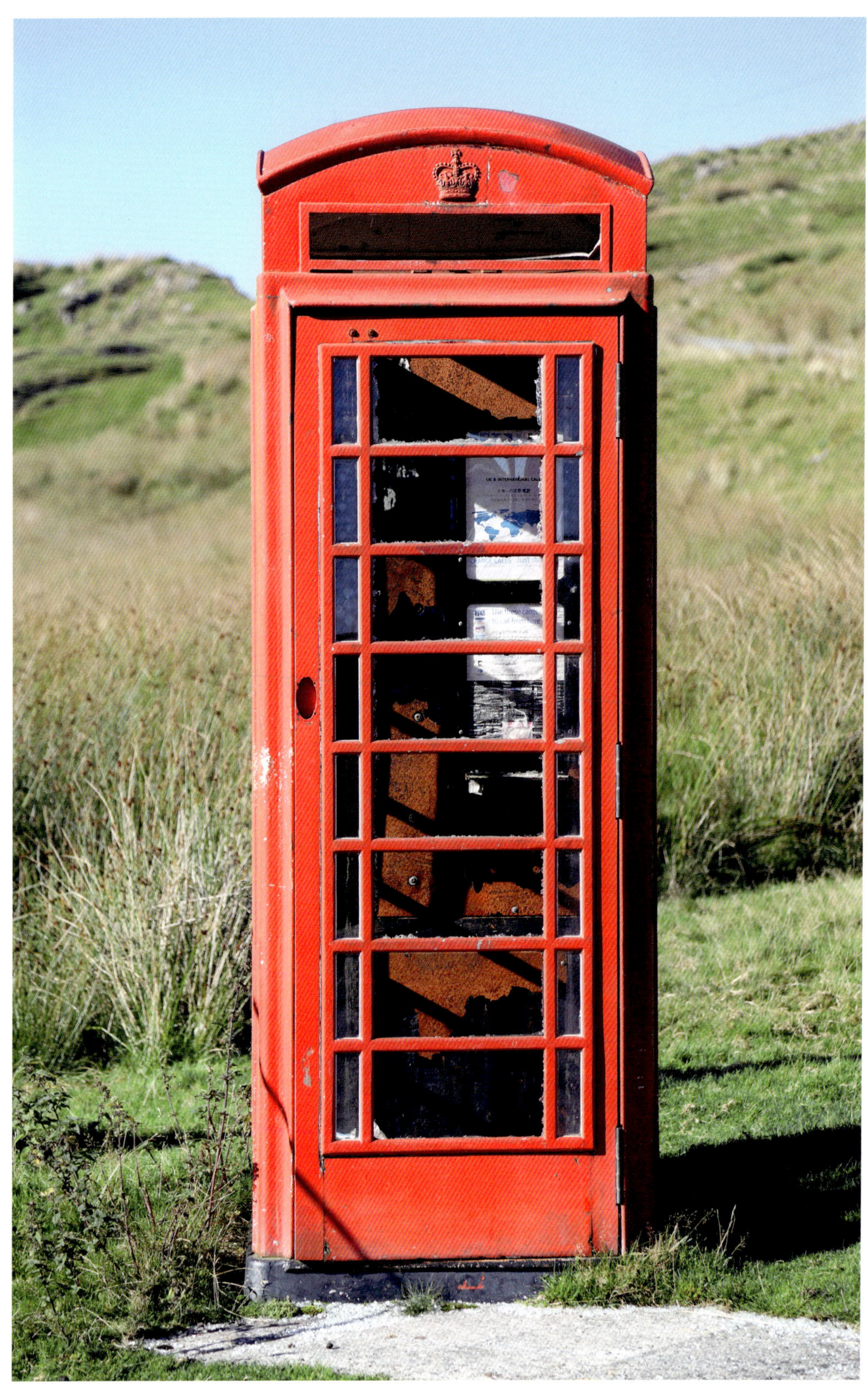

Left: Cambrian Mountains,
Ceredigion, 2011.

Right: Talybont-on-Usk, Powys, 2010.

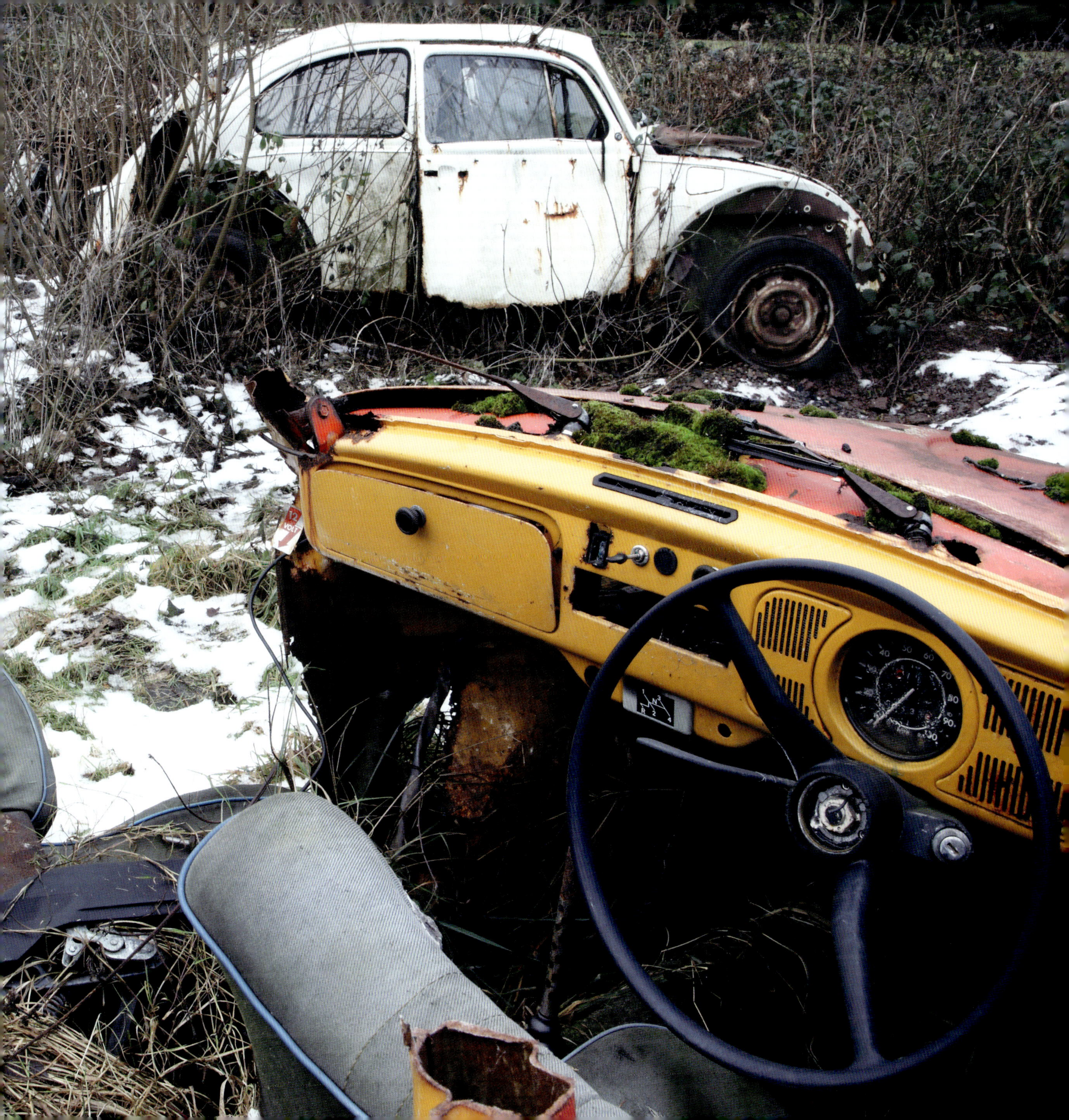

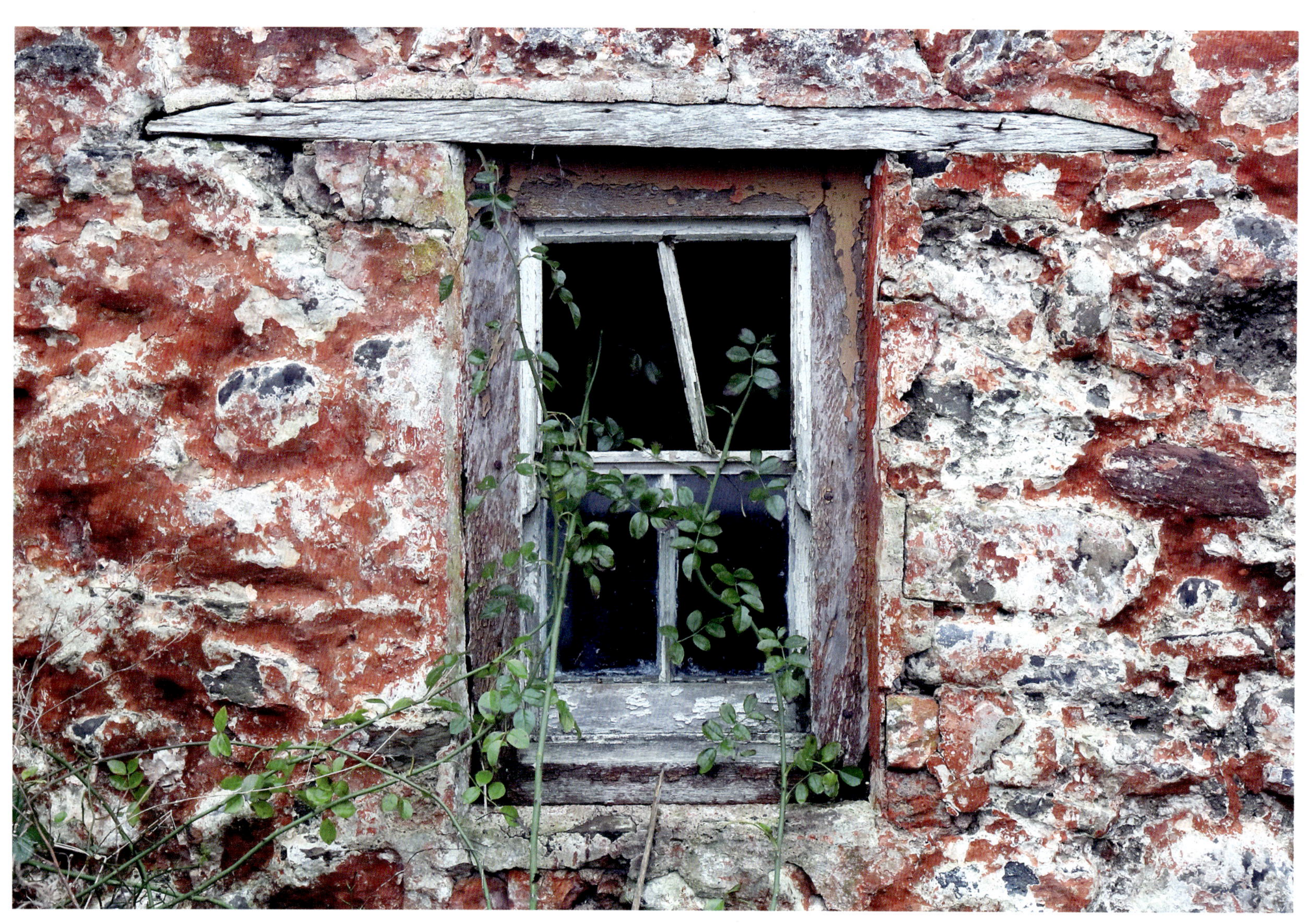

Above: Cresswell Quay, Pembrokeshire, 2022.

Right: Wolfscastle, Pembrokeshire, 2022.

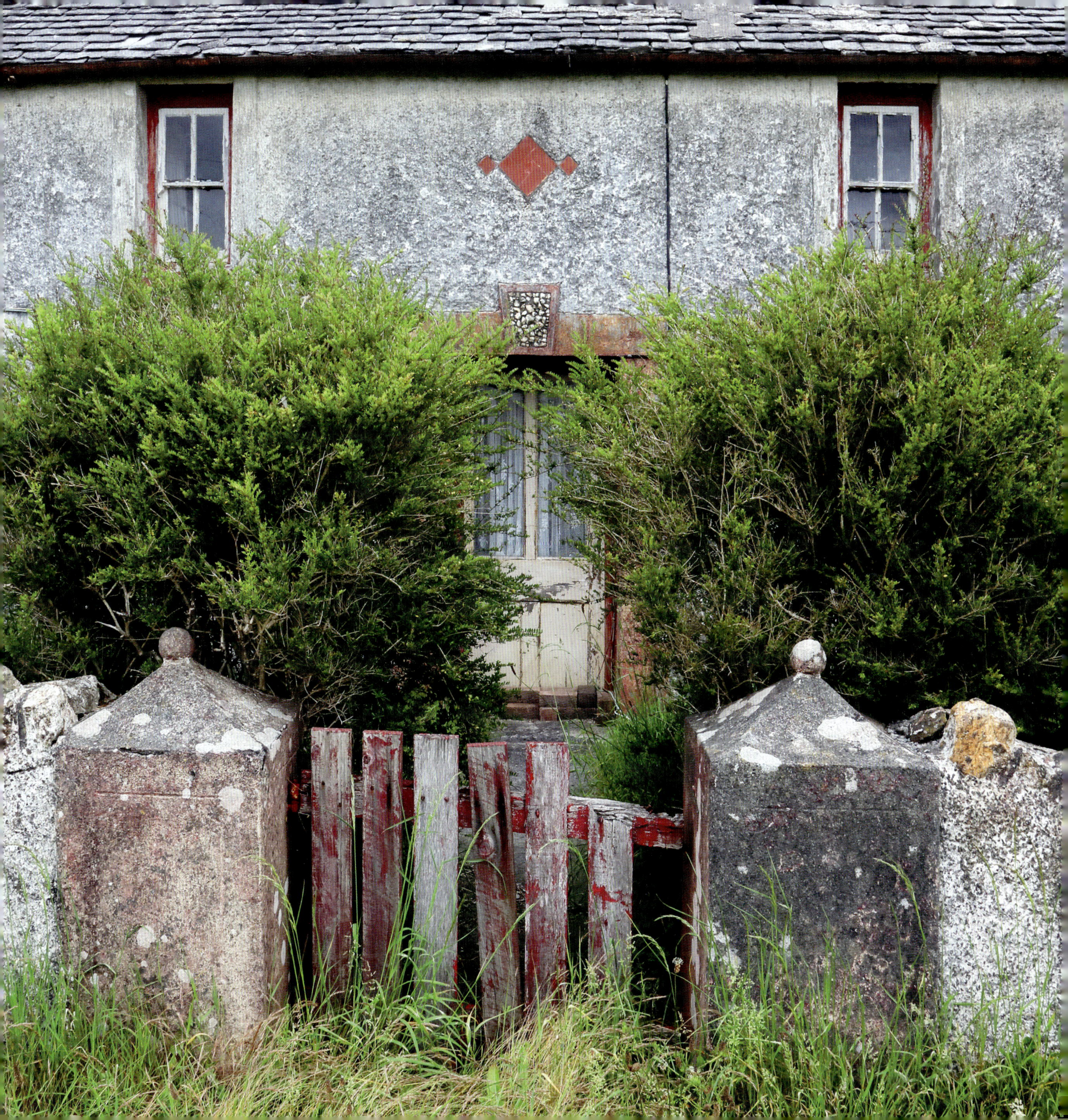

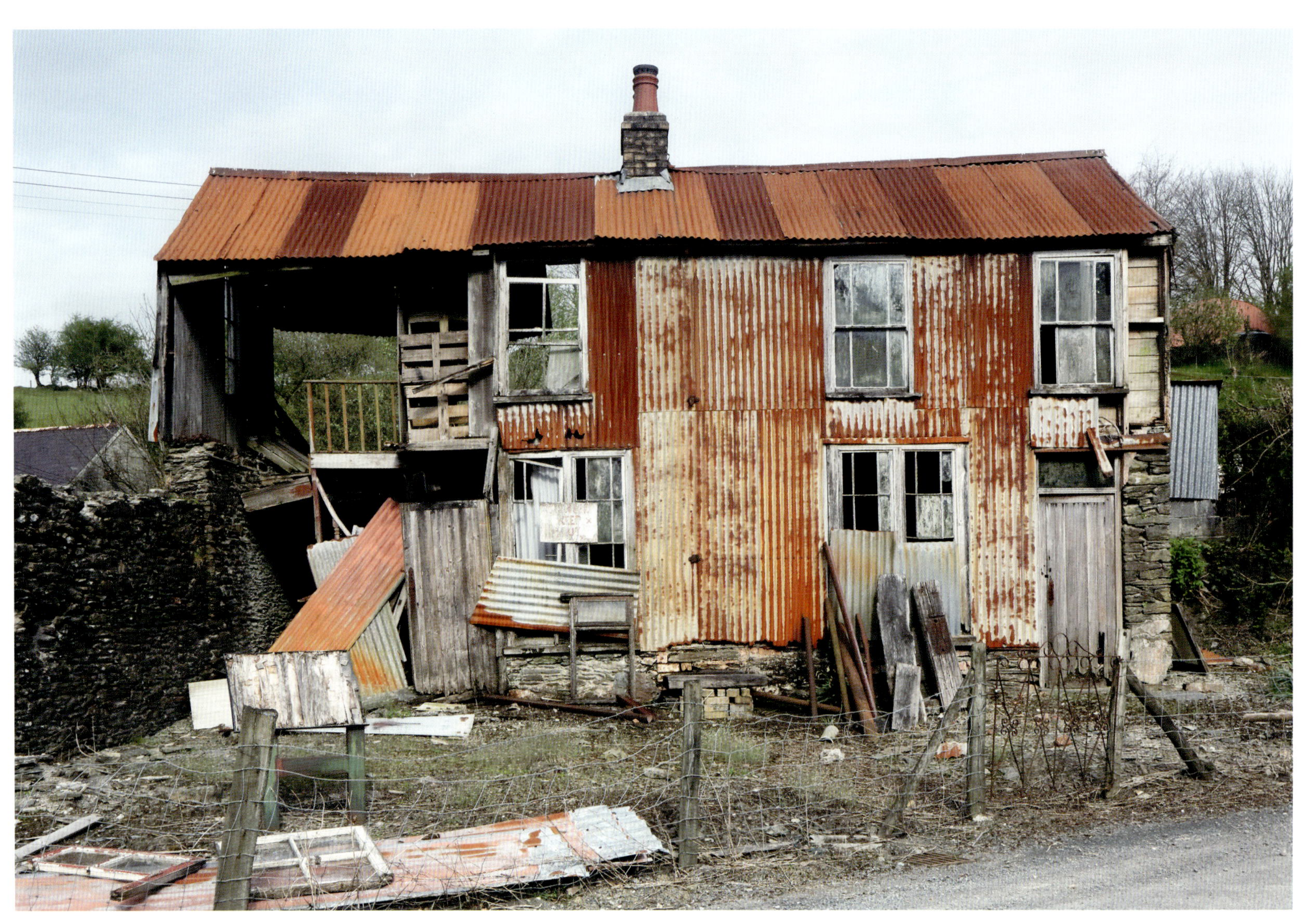

Dinas, Carmarthenshire, 2022.

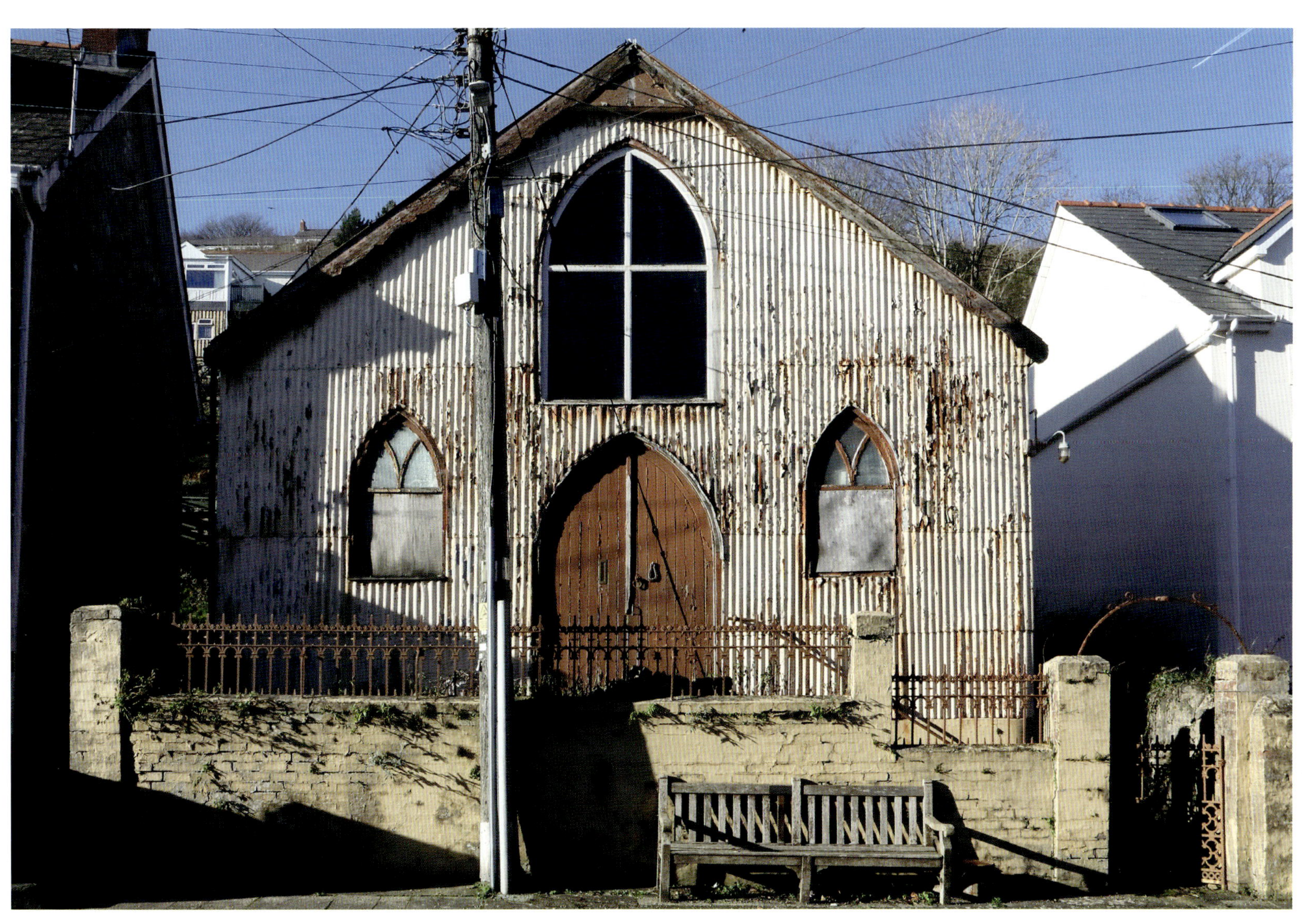

Goodwick, Pembrokeshire, 2023.

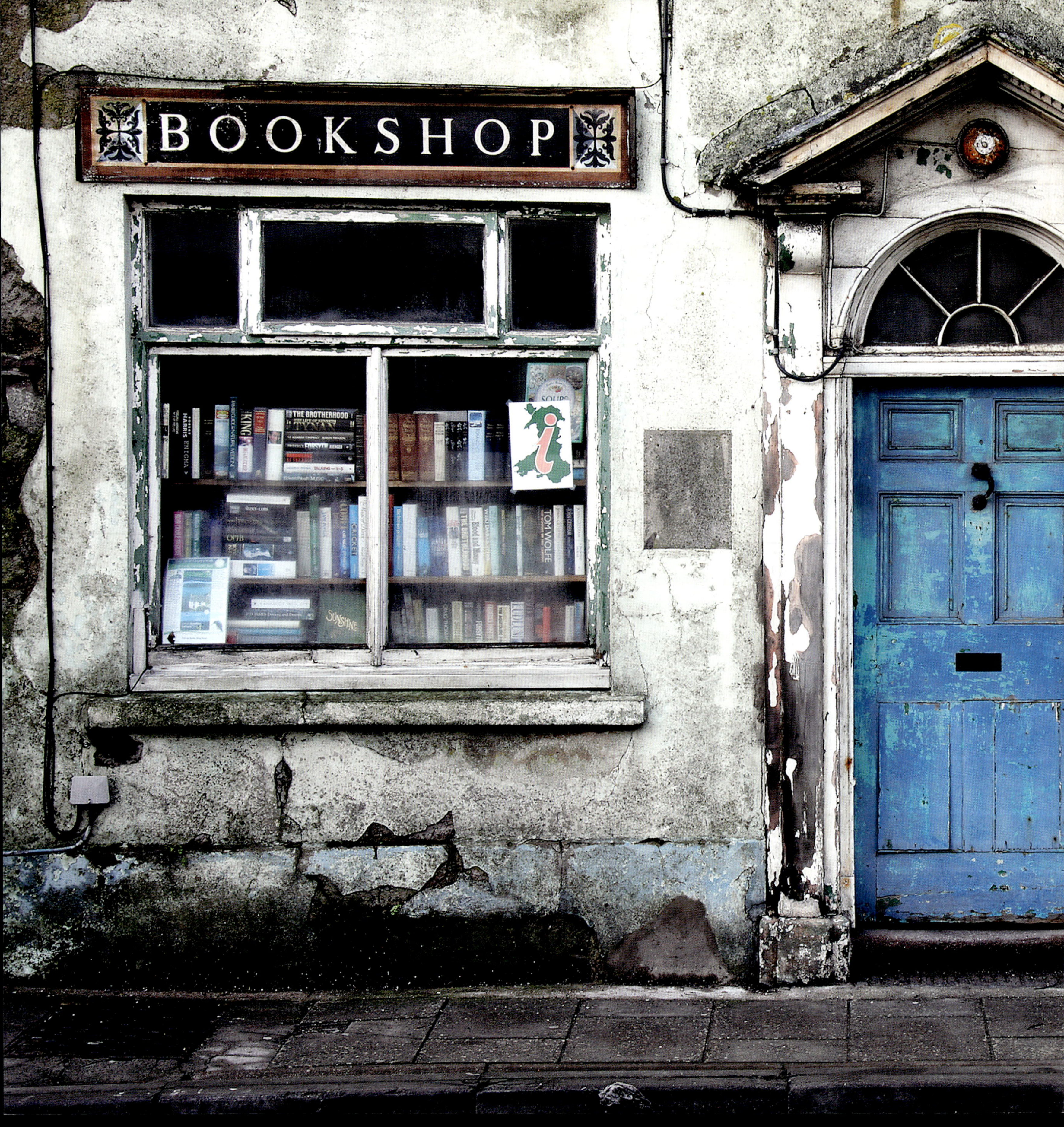
BOOKSHOP

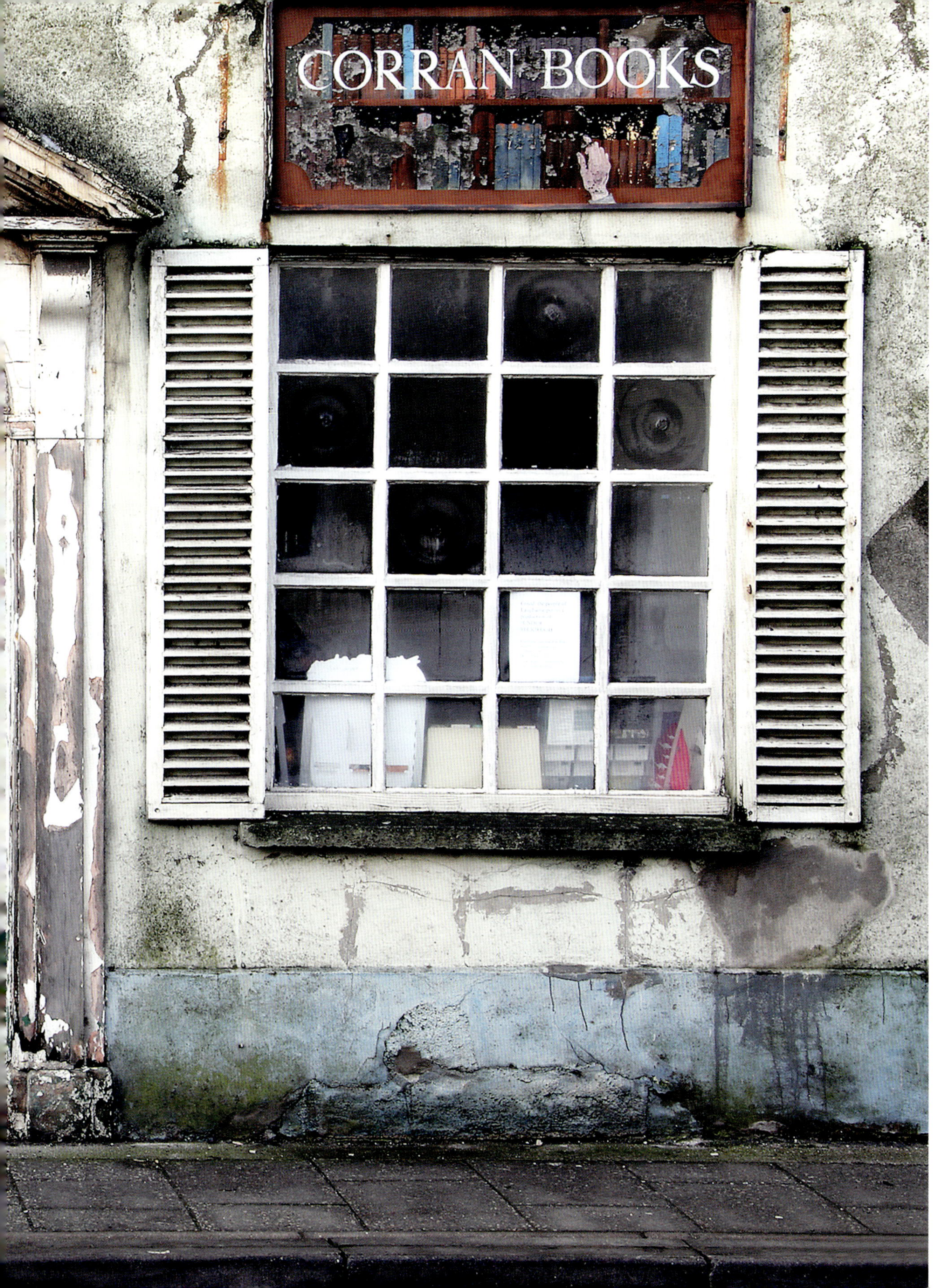

Laugharne,
Carmarthenshire, 2006.

Pages 94-95: Pontiago,
Pembrokeshire, 2006.

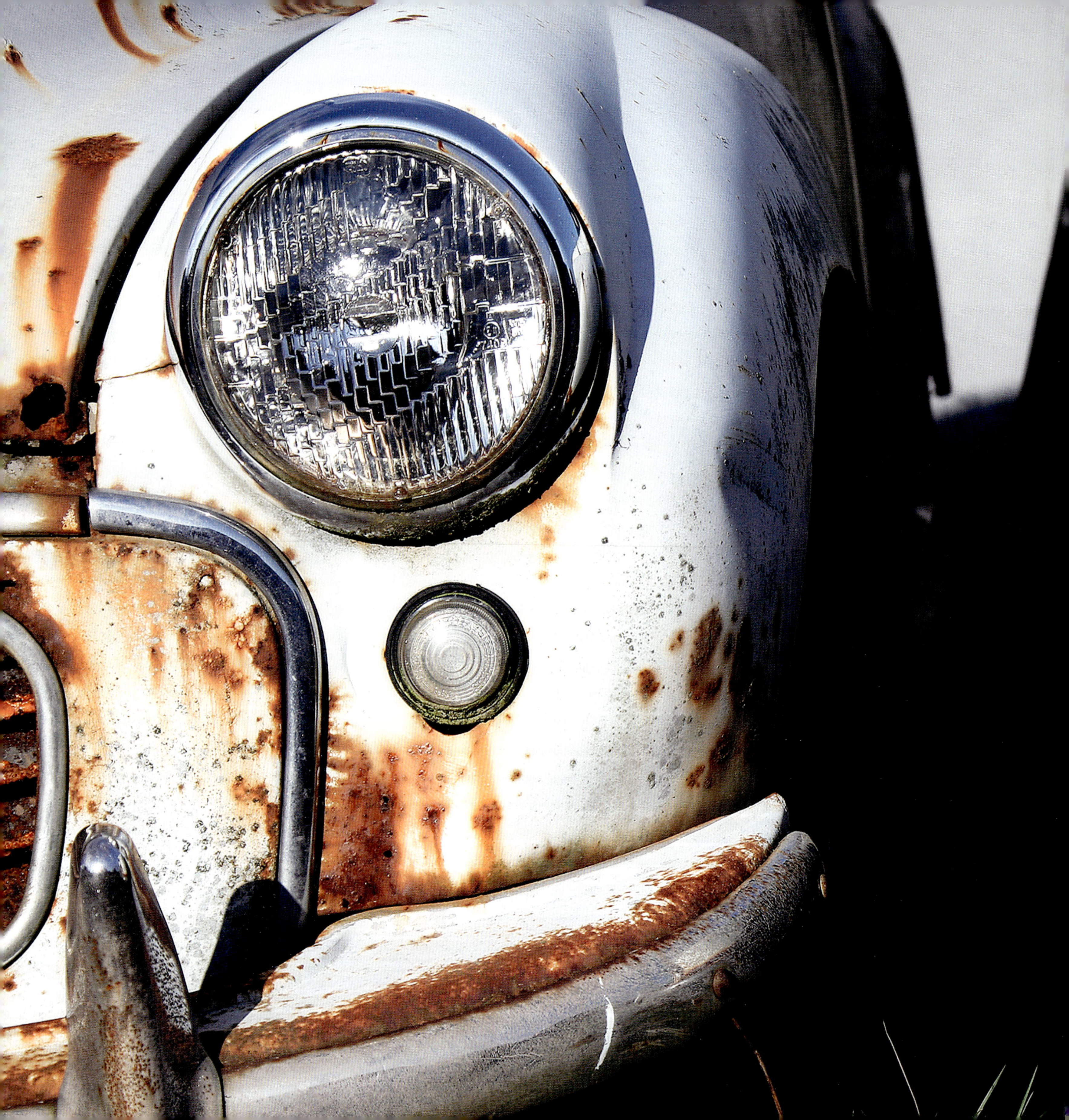

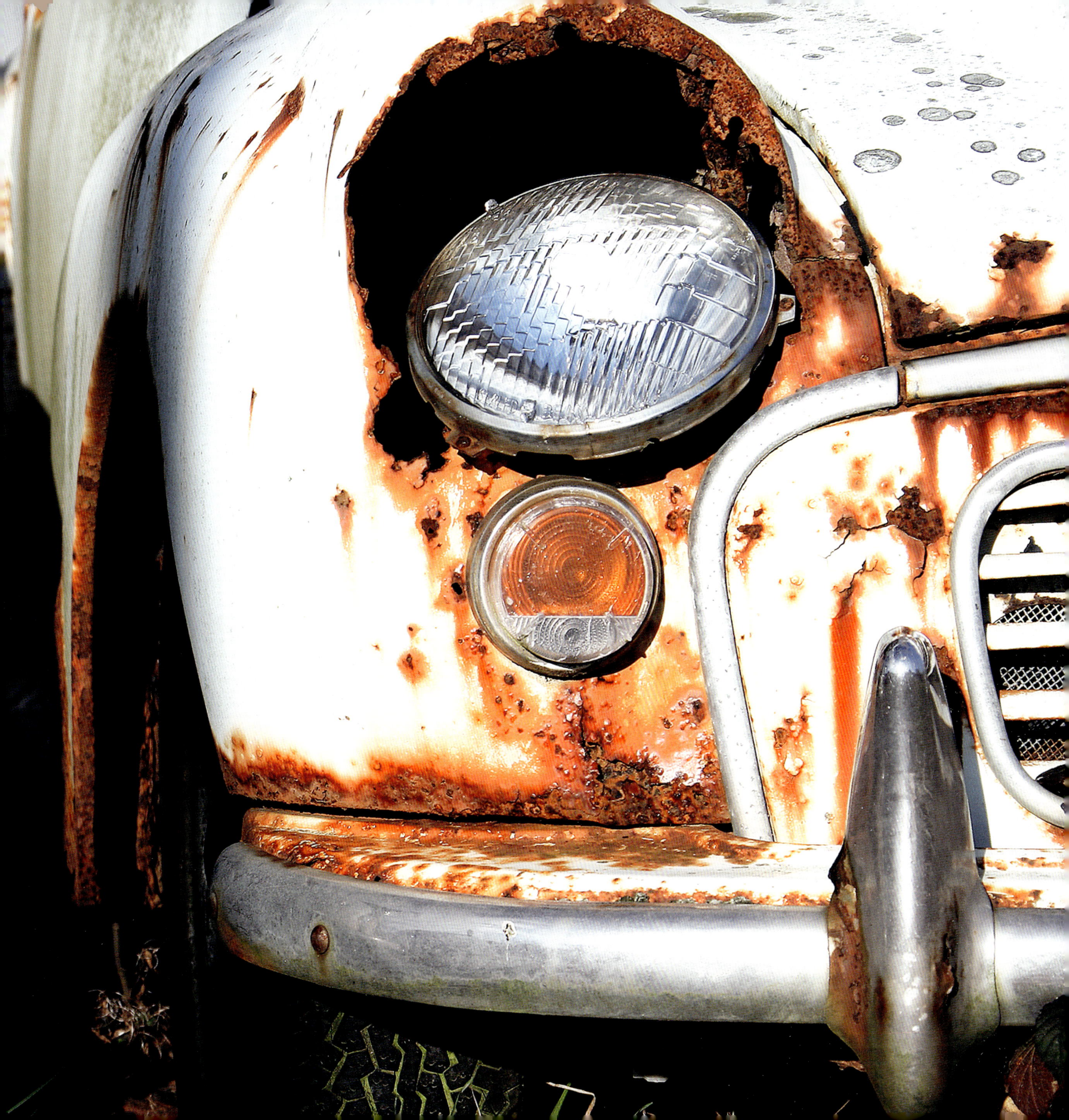

BOOKS BY DAVID WILSON

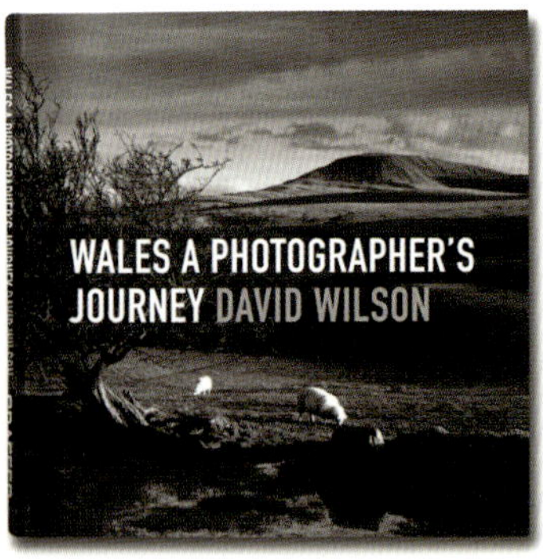

Wales – A Photographer's Journey
- Author David Wilson
- Size 250 x 250mm
- ISBN 9781802580068
- Hardback, 160 pages
- Price £25
- Publication March 2022

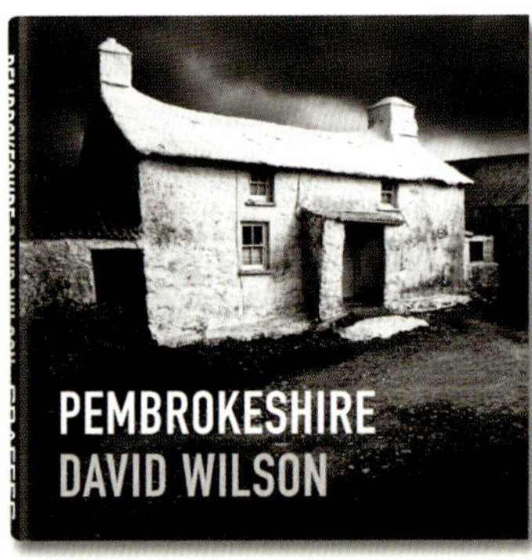

Pembrokeshire
- Author David Wilson
- Size 250 x 250mm
- ISBN 9781802580051
- Hardback, 120 pages
- Price £20
- Publication February 2022

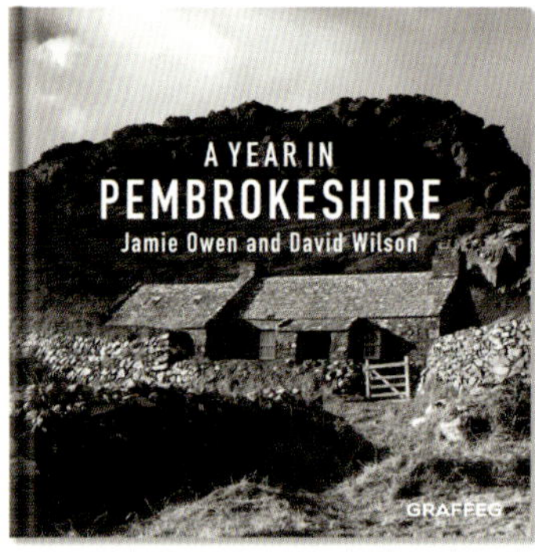

A Year in Pembrokeshire
- Author Jamie Owen
- Photographer David Wilson
- Size 200 x 200mm
- ISBN 9781912213658
- Hardback, 192 pages
- Price £20
- Publication June 2018

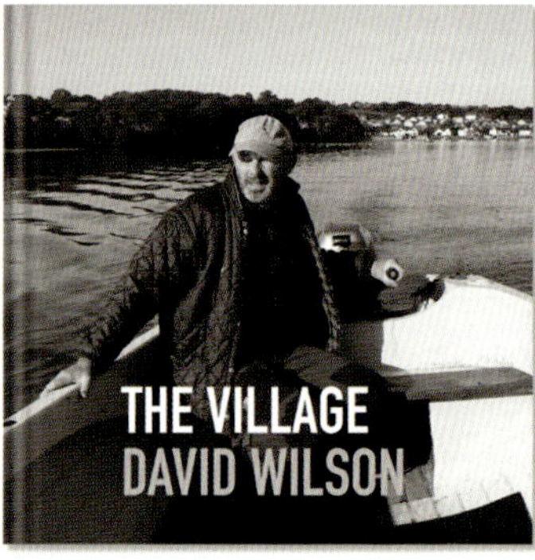

The Village
- Author David Wilson
- Size 200 x 200mm
- ISBN 9781802580488
- Hardback, 128 pages
- Price £20
- Publication November 2021

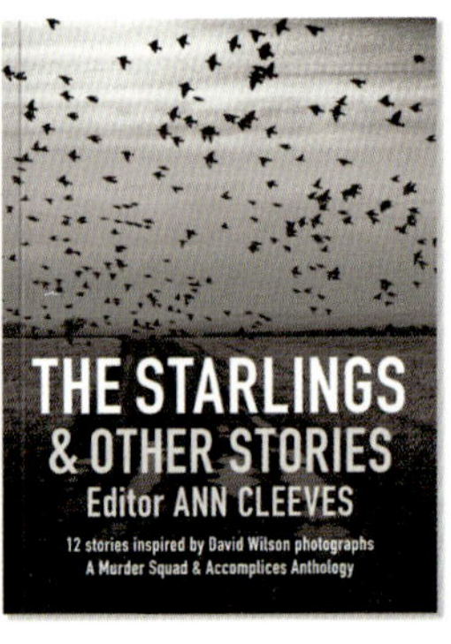

The Starlings & Other Stories
- Editor Ann Cleeves
- Photographer David Wilson
- Size 200 x 150mm
- ISBN 9781909823747
- Hardback, 224 pages
- Price £12.99
- Publication September 2015

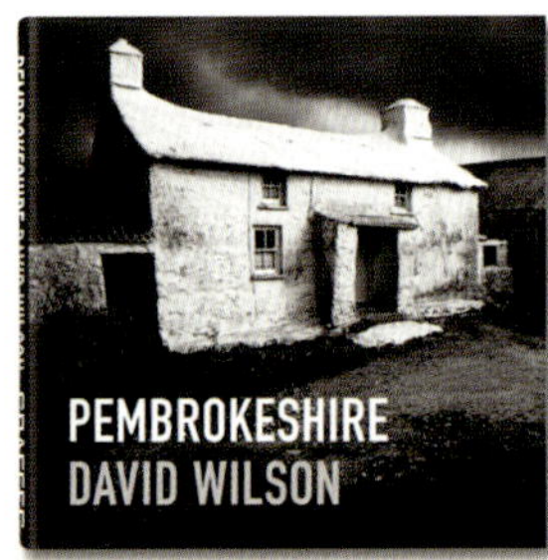

Pembrokeshire Compact edition
- Author David Wilson
- Size 150 x 150mm
- ISBN 9781905582938
- Hardback, 128 pages
- Price £9.99
- Publication August 2013

Peeling Paint and Rust
Published in Great Britain in 2023 by
Bird Eye Books, an imprint of Graffeg
Limited.

Photography and text by David Wilson
copyright © 2023. Designed and
produced by Graffeg Limited copyright
© 2023.

Page 2: Photo of Drew Pritchard © Eleri
Griffiths. Page 4: Photo of David Wilson
© Anna Wilson.

Graffeg Limited, 15 Neptune Court,
Vanguard Way, Cardiff, CF24 5PJ, Wales,
UK. Tel: 01554 824000.
www.graffeg.com.

David Wilson is hereby identified as the
author of this work in accordance with
section 77 of the Copyright, Designs and
Patents Act 1988.

A CIP Catalogue record for this book is
available from the British Library.

ISBN 9781802585681

1 2 3 4 5 6 7 8 9

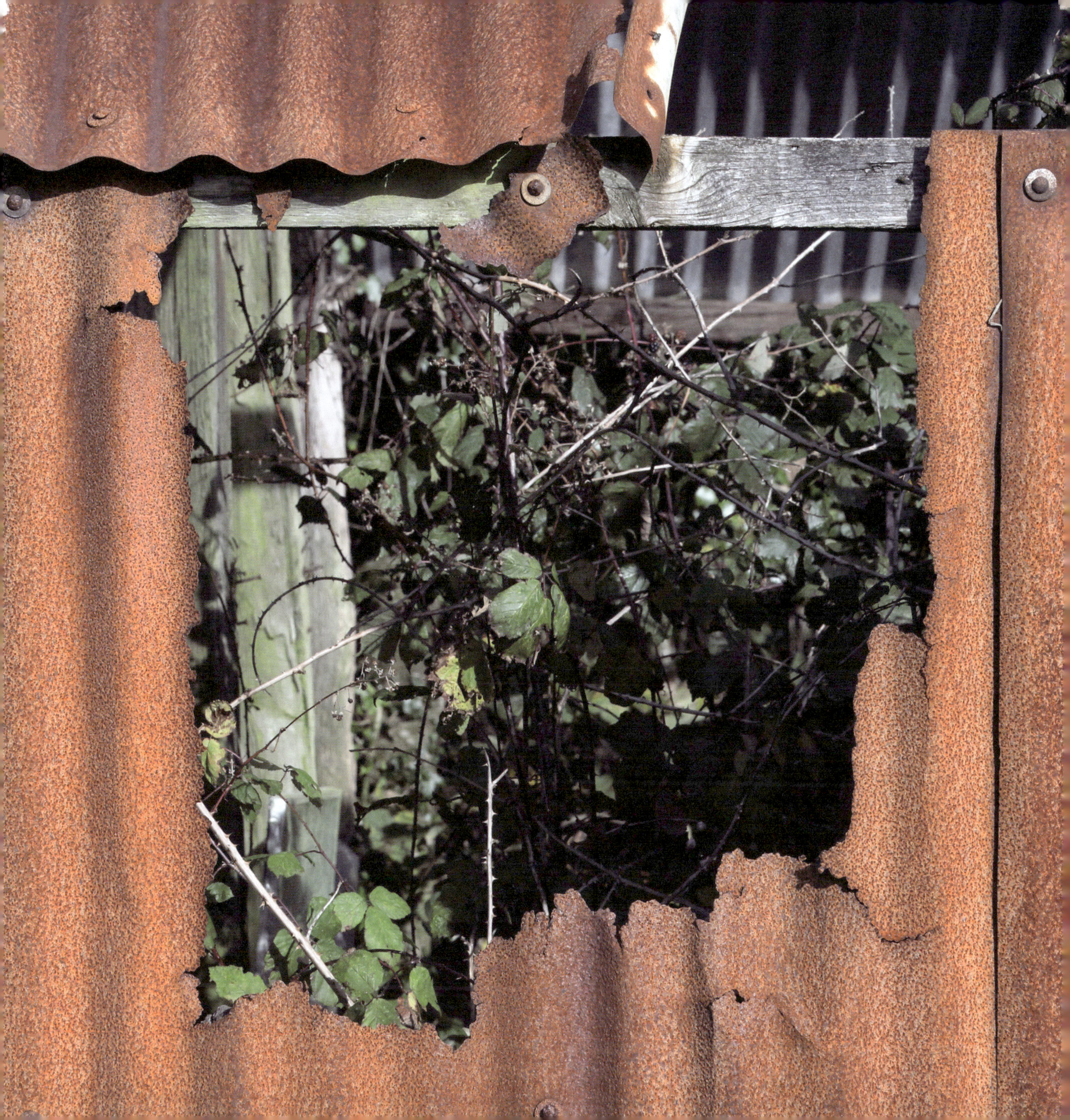